Through The Eyes of The Soul

Expect The Unexpected

Timothy Duncan

AllenRich Publishing
c/o Play Ball Sports Academy
596 Plummer Road
Huntsville, AL 35806

Written by Timothy A. Duncan
Edited by AllenRich Publishing

Photos Courtesy Of: Dokk Savage Film, Music & Photography

Illustrations: Dream Workx Graphix & Signz

Cover Design: Christy Goines Kreashuns Graphics Group

ISBN: 978-0-9993773-0-7

Registration # TXu002019180

The Library of Congress
United States Copyright Office
101 Independence Ave., SE
Washington, D.C. 20559-6000
(202) 707-3000

Printed in the United States of America

Through The Eyes of the Soul

This Book is dedicated to the Memory of

My Heart, My Best Friend, My Everything –

My Mother

Patricia Ann Duncan

Preface

Imagine riding a roller coaster - the speed, turns, and spins - then a sudden stop - and then it all starts again. Imagine the emotions of a man being put on live television for the entire world to see and what that would look like. Imagine finding yourself so wrapped up in emotion then released to fall flat on your face. Imagine laughing and crying at the same time, and seeing the formation of emotion from a distance, and then all of sudden right in your face.

Through the Eyes of the Soul will touch on so many emotions from a man's point of view. Most people that read this book will find themselves as the topic without even trying. You will find yourself wrapped by the words and released with the conclusion. This book will give you an eagle's eye into the emotional state of mind of a man. You will feel the feelings and the emotions in each piece. You will be able to visualize yourself being in that moment, being in that space. It will give you a totally different perspective on how situations and people are viewed at different times in life.

Through the Eyes of the Soul is a reflection of one man's journey through life leading him in many directions and even in the end (still lost to a degree) but at the same time finding himself on many levels. *Through the Eyes of the Soul* reaches depths that most cannot understand. They cannot understand a man being so expressive, so emotional - but we can and we are. Many times it's just not seen, because it's not viewed as strength, but rather as a weakness but there is strength in being able to convey your thoughts to someone, about someone, or in regard to someone or something.

If emotions could tell a story this book will do just that, if words could paint pictures of reality this book will do just that. If words could make fantasy reality this book will do just that. The poems are written in such a way that they transform the mind into a canvas of emotional paints, flowing in all directions creating patterns, elusions, 3D effects or just a picture of sadness, pain, happiness, and peace. This book is life's setbacks and ways forward; it's the beginning of life and the ending of a journey.

Some poems are about the fantasy of pleasing a woman and finding out that pleasure is no longer wanted and having to deal with the emotional side of feeling rejected, feeling turned away by someone you thought loved you or at least they said the words.

Through The Eyes of the Soul poems were inspired by many places. These places include, but are not limited to, real life experiences - where things are not as they seem or they seem wrong but feel so right. Conversations had - whether short or long - but the point was made to put pin to paper as that conversation needed to be talked out further ......and so now the world will be able to pierce into my interpretation of that conversation.

"I write about what I see, hear, think, and feel" - Tim Duncan

For You...

For you I put pen to paper, for you I put my emotions on display as the rays from the sun reflect from my eyes the truth as I see it and you will feel it and be able to connect to it. The Purple Tear of Royalty represents my joys, my pains, my ups as well as my downs, for it flows as a gift given to me to give to you - for a novelty it's not, but I give all I got to and for you. So I thank you from the deepest part of my soul for even wanting to explore my passion as nothing is left to ration out for I pour out all. My family, my friends and my supporters whether near or far, you will always be the twinkle in my eye as you explore Through The Eyes of the Soul.

Table of Contents

Part I - Through

Part II – The Eyes

Through The Eyes of the Soul

Through The Eyes of the Soul

Part III – The Soul

Through The Eyes of the Soul

Through The Eyes of the Soul

Part I

Through

... I see through the eyes of unlimited possibility, no matter how many times you fall "I See You"

Rest In Peace my Brother

I still miss you daily, some days are long and dreadful
Not willing to face reality.
Rest In Peace my Brother
for today is our day, we celebrate our birth but I mourn your death. Not
a day goes by that I wish you had one more breathe, so we could hang
out and talk of new and old times. Wish you could see your girls and
how much they've grown; they miss you like I do for all the love shown.
Thinking of those times when all three Duncan boys were singing the
song I'll rise again but not knowing we would be separated so soon,
so I wait until that time when you rise again. Years gone by but still
feels like yesterday when I received the call of your last day, But
Rest In Peace my Brother
for its Peace that I strive and long for, from the times we were boys set
to be men expected to achieve greatness, not in the way that most
perceive but be able to receive greatness for we were destined to know
the power of treating others the way we want to be treated.
A Mother's love
and
A Father's guidance
to a path set forth.....

Rest In Peace my Brother
I miss you Bro ... Happy BDay

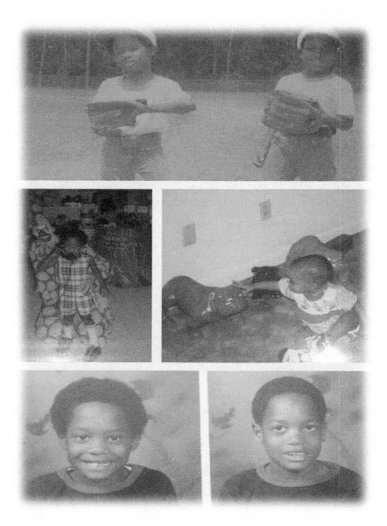

Through The Eyes of the Soul

Walk with Me!

Why does time no longer remain, I just wanted.to walk and talk and feel the breeze but now I'm on bended knee asking for guidance on this road less traveled. Can time stand still so we can talk about life and what the prospects looks like. Can we reflect on the past to enhance the present to look forward to the future? Can we argue as friends and at the end love like brothers? Hey slow down, you act like you have somewhere to go, let's take our time and clear our minds and talk this thing out, even if we have to cry this thing out, we will get this thing out. Why again are you walking so fast, is there a task that requires your immediate attention and you failed to mention how life had been treating lately because we share like that and place our cares, our fears, our trust in each other like that, Now I'm chasing you, you are moving too fast, this pace I can't keep up, you are out of my grasp, so do I let go to hold on or do I hold on that much tighter to the memories as they are more precious than gold. My heart aches but beats for life as we knew it, if another picture could have been painted with your own blood you would have drew it. So I stand affirmed and I stand determined to live the life we were destined for as destiny will have it and it is so said in the word, you will hear a voice to say get up and I'll be right there to welcome you back with open arms of joy and amazement and immediately ask "Will you walk with me". Just as your soul will be an ever gleaming light to my pathway as I still walk with you and talk with you and your existence will never cease to exist.
T.D.

Through The Eyes of the Soul

Gone but not forgotten

Seasons change, winter to spring, hot to cold,
you're not forgotten your soul my soul. A
bond never broken our souls intertwine,
yours all wrapped up in mine. You may be
gone but you're not forgotten. Joy unleashed
when I think of your smile, the thought of
you always, not just a little while. I live in you
and you in me and GOD almighty so that
makes three. Days too few, weeks too long,
years gone by, the thought still holds strong.
Your memory so fresh still on my mind did GOD say stop and
hold up time.
I view your face when last we talked, the times we sang, the times
we walked.
Angels watch over me as they watch over you, words of inspiration,
and no passions to subdue.
Will to live and carryon, you may be gone but your face still appears
like yesterday, you block all dangers that come my way. So thankful
for yesterday just blessed to see today, for some never seen for most
never heard, it comes like a thief not saying a word. I'm talking
about tomorrow.

Go for it, go jump to it, go get on it, go do what you will to it just
don't hurt it, beat it with tenderness, trample it with kindness, step
on it with all your might and try to break it.
Hold it in your hands and watch it beat ever so slowly, squeeze it
until the veins start to appear, twist and turn with it changing up the
gear.
Put it between your thighs and feel it throb like a vibrator, caressing
you, comforting your innermost beauty, it's my duty to ensure
you're completely compelled with the openness of mind and body.
Put it under your feet if you want to feel empowered, hold it high
above your head and let it shower you with juices of goodness.
You can store it away or keep it close for easy access; you can put in
the corner and keep an eye of it while you undress.
You can talk to it and expect a reply, you can scream at it and
emotions it won't deny, you can cry on it and lay all your worries
there, you can sleep on it and worries be no more.
Stay focused, keep an open mind,
I'm talking about my heart.

My Granny My Anchor

Even through tossed and driven by the waves of
life, she gave words of wisdom despite the strife.
Her words so gently spoken, not a negative one
even touched her lips. Her hands always giving not
wanting a single thing back.
Because of her way my values and character had a solid
foundation, she made me feel I could conquer anything not
limiting the nation. She would always say treat people good and
good comes back to you, sometimes I even wonder do people
really have a clue.
A clue as to what being Christ like really is, let Granny tell it, it
is what it is.
Granny endured all trails without the bat of an eye; her faith
touched every life from young to old.
Her words of wisdom and encouragement were something
to behold.
My heart and soul so deeply touched by 92 years of service to
family, church and community to say the least.
Granny I will see you later in God's paradise where we will sit
together again as family at God's wonderful feast.
Granny I love you and I will say again see you later.
8/4/07

Through The Eyes of the Soul

Sometimes

Sometimes I get caught in the middle of my own thoughts trying to figure out which direction is the correct path but narrow is the way, success and failure's road has many lanes so here I stand wanting to make a move but my first has to be right for there is no turning back, be that as it may, I just may fall on my face only to realize in the dirt is not where I want to be so I get up on my knees, face dusty, sweat running down my brow, only making it more difficult to see so I depend on faith and the journey continues. Traveling graces and your prayers guide me daily, comforting thoughts of memories gone by but resurrected in an instant to bring sunshine on a cloudy day. Even though battered and bruised from life's constant blows of unexpectedness, your presence I feel massaging the pain away to keep moving forward. Forward I crawl because right now too weak to stand, forward I crawl to a destination of uncertainties, murky waters where the visibility is nonexistent but I depend on your guidance, I depend on your vision to lead me to a place of peace and release all the stresses of life so I can stand again to further continue my journey.

DEDICATED TO MY MOTHER, NOT JUST FOR MOTHER'S DAY BUT EVERYDAY .... MISS YOU!

Through The Eyes of the Soul

dam them mountains

as i look not over Jordan, over the plains i see all,

even further than the all-seeing eye.

the snowcaps represent your soul covered oh so slightly but open only to those that dare to explore your innermost mystery.

only to find something more beautiful than the clearest diamond, or a well carved rock.

damn them mountains, you walk up one and you think their all just the same,

remember they were formed and all have a name.

the trails are your mind, your thoughts are but one, your body's like a spring as the waters run.

your waters flow, so delicious to my lips as i imagine that place where I can be free.

it's them dam mountains again letting me be me.

You let go

All was in front of you starring you right in face but without a trace you place the tune for dismissal and no reversal of thoughts or your feeling were never seen again. I still see and smell traces of you from the place you once laid but betrayed by the contemplation of manipulation I safeguarded what I thought was my heart, be it unprotected it still rejected the notion of repeal, yet and still I tried but lied to myself thinking it was anything clever, only foolish for thoughts and fears and much needed tears to drain off the fluid of a burden down soul so cold now warm with new life of trust a must to move forward to a destination still to be determined not by us but us separately hoping our paths come this way again. You let go, now free to decree newest of spirit and expressions of selflessness ... so long I'm gone.

Internal Monologue Thoughts...

Easy to give up on years of passion and pain,
sunshine and rain only to gain nothing of a world which has
offered back that which was given but took me to a place that I
thought was me but not me, give me back so I can give back to the
one that needs me most like my host feeding off my every drip of
joy and aspiration even though frustration sits there waiting to take
hold as I hold on to the ledge of destiny yes our destiny, our legacy
to be true and last, last longer than this storm of me finding who I
once was then who I am to judge me for I see not my faults but
yours but glorify mine therefore I shine not as a diamond but as
solid rock for you to stand as I bend and lift you higher. I create
failures with success only to be trumped by selfish desires and fires
of oppression which have taken my cries and turned them into
screams for help as I lean not on your shoulder but your breast for
it nurtures my being from corrupting all I am to never return as I
was but I like who I am and will never change.

A Storm Like You

Wind and rain rage all night long; trees begin to fall even though
their strong.
A quick burst of sunshine came just as the day breaks,
the storm was not over flooding rivers, flooding lakes.
All of a sudden a calm with no interruption,
a storm like you can cause total destruction.
It's best to lay low and let it pass, the harder you fight it the longer it last.
Excessive wind and explosive rain all but a storm feeling my pain. The
storm of life has taught me so much; don't lean on man for he's not a
crutch, you lean on him you can't help but fall, lean on GOD an
unmovable wall.
This wall of faith will never shatter just lean on him he'll solve the
matter.

<u>Confusion</u>

Putting my thoughts together is not an easy task; it's like Halloween and
wearing a mask.
The nights are so dark and the sun never seems to shine, it seems
like darkness almost all the time.
But having a friend brings a sparkle of light and the nights seem
shorter at the close of the night.
The days seem longer with the sun shining so bright with help from up
above I get through the night. The nights are not as long as they used to
be, with help from up above and love for me.
Love for myself had almost diminished with love for others it was
soon replenished.
How can I respect the world when there's no respect for me,
I'm like a grain of sand in a deep blue sea?

Slow Down

Slow down girl, you're moving too fast.
I just saw your face now I see your ass.
Don't move too fast, I won't fight the feeling,
if its three years later I'll still be willing, willing
to caress your soft red lips, massage your soft
brown hips.
Don't rush it baby the time will come, I'll make love to you and say
you're the one.
But if you move too fast I see your face and now your ass.
You'll say I came to quick, I did not lick, I just wanted to stick and I
make you sick, you might even say I have a short dick.
But if you slow your roll and take control of your body not mine,
I'm in control but the direction you charted,
off course before we started someone ends up broken hearted
because you moved too fast,
I saw your face then I saw your ass.
Slow Down.

PAIN!!!

How much more pain will I have to bare before I throw up
my hands and not even care.
Not wanting to love or ever feel again, do I put myself in the ranks
of all other men?
Do I put myself down like a lizard or a snake because of my
broken heart from an untrue mate?
My standards are too high to ever go that low, respect for myself will
never let it show.
Things might be bad but they could always be worst, just stay on
your knees and keep GOD first.
My pain runs deep I can't even trace it, trying to run from it
and soon will have to face it.
My pain runs deep to the core of the earth, I wonder did it start
the day of my birth,
I wonder did it start the day we met.
It probably began that day we parted, the love was lost and then
the pain started.
When will it stop? When will it stop?
This question couldn't be answered by many or few, if anyone
has the answer could it be you?
Maybe I have the answer it's deeper than I thought it's just like
love it can be bought.

Today is Tomorrow

Today is tomorrow what holds us back?
The thought of today often brings sorrow, my sorrow so deep the
mind too complex bringing about madness then what comes
next. My sorrow not worried but may be concerned, my sorrow
takes over but my soul still yearns, yearning for something
beyond your wildest dream. The being of happiness, peace, and
joy.
Be that strong black monument not a cheap bought toy.
The stillness overcome as the day break rises, life too demanding
so full of compromises. I won't compromise but soon I will wake.
Life still the same with so much at stake. If I had to settle for what
life had to give I would soon be consumed and could not live. Give
me morals and values to say the least to be consumed by it all I
would become a beast. My actions true examples of the one life I
lead, my words testimony or just talk of a deed. A word not spoken
is more misunderstood, too many words spoken will do me little
good.
2/18/97

Baby, Baby, Baby

Say baby, hey baby what's yo malfunction
What makes you function that's the question?
Bring me joy bring me pain bring me sunshine after the rain.
Today too soon, yesterday too late my ills are few my love won't wait.
Save the best for last because I'll be home soon not too late not too soon.
Stars of aspiration give me hope, a star shines at night but when day comes you know it's still there just like me no replacement and none like it. Just know I'm here to stay whether night or day. I never watch you sleep you always watch me, like a shining star; just like me no replacement and none like it.

Can I, Will I, I Won't

Can I get tired of waking up next to you, caressing you, and you saying stop but really mean go, so I continue and like always the panties drop. Will I get tired of your honesty so bold, sometimes it hurts but it heals my soul? A soul lost for so long wondering here and there not knowing where to rest for it may be a test, a game, we are too grown for those but you have lit my fire. A fire of desire for you and no one else, no one compares, the stares that were once glances.

The touches that are now caresses, I undress you with my eyes now all is physically removed, sounds turn into music, the way you communicate, the way you move.

Can I get or be confused by all these emotions and feeling and treat these two competitors just the same, or do I treat them with respect and give them their honest name.

Will I continue to love you with all I am, no flowing rivers, just a built up dam, holding all this goodness ready to be unleashed.

I can't worry much about whether one day you will say I can take no more, I will live in the moment where happiness dwells most, sipping mimosas, and eating fruit off the eastern coast. If today were our last and tomorrow cease to exist, I can honestly say I won't. Sitting here hoping for a happy ending, is there one to be had because after all its the ending of everything.

Broken Pieces

Purpose for life when it should have been taken, with tears of joy to my knees I'm shaken. From infant years to grown up days I find myself standing in the way of shame and my name means the same for I have taken hold of my own truth. PTSD how when military service is nonexistent on any record I hold but a hold on my childhood it has as my mind has been ravaged and plagued by warlike symptoms that memories had were lost and replaced by dramatic screams and blood soaked visions of a past even though forgiven still cannot give life to a life I want so bad to remember as ones around me reflect I can only detect from facial expressions that I'm part of the story being told so I react to not detract away from the excitement and I wonder was that really me and pictures prove the latter but the only thing I see is blood splatters on the walls so I regress for the test I was given I forgot the answers a long time ago. Broken Pieces are my life at times when eyes were laid on an unfamiliar face, starting with an introduction of name not knowing I was the trophy piece at the end of game. Detailed conversations had, for it seemed that my words, my stories of life transcending belief that Fairytale love did exist and it was sealed with a kiss so intoxicating as I begin hallucinating that I was in all too familiar place but a not so familiar face for they had changed and my mind became rearranged as I only wanted another drink, another sip as I dipped into some sheets only to wake to daybreak for I took another look and there amazed at the audacity to let me sleep that long.
T.D.

How can I?

How can I explain or even try to remain focused not on you, but us,
as we move out of the distance?
I want to go but you say no I can do it on my own,
I have shown not only you but others I can do it. I never questioned
your ability nor your-know-how.
It's amazing how fast you have relocated away from me.
Dam I miss you and you're not even gone. It hurts a little all the way
down to the bone. I knew it was a reason I tried to stay away, for this
feeling of falling in love and have to feel this way. Why can't I help you
achieve your goals, I have gone this far with nowhere to turn but I turn
to do what I do best, which is smile and continue to move forward with
my head high, eyes front, yes focused my journey alone but not in vain,
many tears on my face, you can't see for the down pour of rain.

———————————————————

Is that what it is?

I sit around wondering what your day holds and as time unfolds I remained focused not on the task at hand but the clock how it winds, moving ever slower by each devastating moment. I find my impatient as patience has no virtue, holding back words hoping not to hurt you. Now this patience thing, yeah we are distant foes trying to become closer is work in progress, some days I do well the others I regress. I Don't Act This Way, I'm always cool just sitting back as the flock begins to gather then I walk down and pick the best out the bunch. Will we do breakfast? No I think lunch. I want to get to know you and the qualities you possess, not running game and surely not a test. My way is my way as it always seems, my dreams your reality and still not enough as I peel back layers, see I'm not so tough. I just want respect as all real Men do, you could walk way today and all but do you. My patience is thin I'm trying to add flavor to thicken it up so the aroma you savor. I feel you deep, despite the shortness of time, I feel you closer as our thoughts intertwine. Do I take a step back before my thoughts get off track or do I continue forward and attack, attack? Each option is considered with my mind at ease, a gentle breeze. I can see clearly now that my thoughts are no longer confused, I have viewed you at all angles at each I remain amused, excited, flabbergasted are words just to name a few, is it you or the things you do. Compatibility unparalleled, conversation flawlessly frayed with gentle hints of smiles, laughter and all the things in between, I find myself thinking is this really a dream. I wake to reality and you are still there, I look into your eyes and try not to stare. I write down my thoughts to pass my existence, I indulge myself in work to fight off resistance. The resistance, not to think of you but to think of you and not stop my existence ....

Occupied

Am I a stranger to myself not knowing which way to turn, am I wrong for feeling this way when love and acceptance is all I yearn. I fault myself for being this way, tripped and fell again for the same game that got me before. I fault myself for caring when no one else did; I fault myself for sharing when no one else would. I fault myself for not standing with my strong back braced for any attack, for lack thereof I am now on my back. As I stand, maybe slower than others would like, but like my determination to get up and fight and avoid all the pitfalls of what you would call failure. I have decided to demand redemption for myself never giving up on me and who I am. I will rise up from these ashes which have scared me more than life itself. I will rise from these ashes and find my true self amongst the clouds. I will soar with eagles to rescue not devour my misconceived notions about myself and restore them to greatness as I am. Beat down, torn up, and yet still I rise. Misunderstood, hoping and wishing I could, still I rise. Still I rise to be me and no one else.

Can I be myself

Can I be myself whether childish or serious, can I be myself and not have to worry about being judged and taken for granted because of some so called sensitive words that have been conveyed across to you as weakness. Whether you know it or not strength lies in those words, whether you know it or not compassion lies in those words, most importantly a part of me lies on top of all those words. I speak candidly about my feeling, leaving nothing more to the imagination than hopes and desires. I speak heartfelt truth in my words, hurt comes out and you can see it clearly, hurt comes out can't you see I miss you dearly. I possess only what has been given me, I only take what is granted to me, with your permission I ask for you, but my questions go unanswered, my inquires go without response, nothing left to do but be myself. I create distance for needed breathing room, I build up walls for construction in progress, danger zones don't enter here; don't come this way, not responsible for what may take place if you try to deconstruct this wall. Can I be myself, laughing, joking, smiles complete with some unfamiliar facial expressions, even some physical gestures displaying my desire for you. Can I be myself, reaching out to you to hold and caress you, looking into your eyes deeper than you have ever experienced. Can I be myself, wanting to make your dreams come true, trying my best to satisfy your every want, trying my best to make sure you carve no one else but me, trying my best to give you the best part of me?
Can I be myself and you accept it?

A Man's Creed

I promise to give you the moon if you provide the stars. I promise
diamonds and pearls if you promise to be my best friend forever. I
promise passion every day when I see your face, I promise to smile
every day when I see your face. I promise to treat your body as my own,
for you know I love myself therefore making it extremely easy to love
you back. I promise to turn your cries of pain to moans of satisfaction,
just give me your heart, I love a fatal attraction. Death do us part for we
will never part ways, just part back the sheets as we undercover and
explore every facet of our fascination with each other. You are my lover,
my friend, a true companion, we are the boys when we hang out or the
girls sitting at home watching a flick maybe not desired too much, but
it's not the content of the film that keeps our attention but the company
next to us that's keeps our attention. Our promises are our soon to be
actions, our promises not filled in time often cause a not so positive
reaction. Patience I grant you, just grant me the same, let me prove
you're wrong so I can be right, timeline still not met so here comes the
fight. The fight for dominance, who's more important, who's on top or
bottom, no one wins, we both end up losing, with scars to prove we won
nothing but distance when closeness should have been our motivator.

Flowing Thoughts...

Let go of the past for it no longer has a place in the present, it has
served its purpose building a stronger more confident me. Let go of the
past and just live in moment, no worries to think about just live in the
moment but the moment you reminisce on that first kiss or the first
pounding of a fist you regress to not be your best and set on a quest to
figure out what went wrong, it all did and once accepted in mind, your
body will follow not making the same mistakes, nor having any regrets
about the past only to move forward from those events not of
circumstance more of coincidence. Circumstance and coincidence have
you here in this place at this time making time for you as you see that
there is something more to see, more to receive, more to give as you
live and let go and move forward not looking back but glancing over
your shoulder with a smile to say thank you. No remorse, just thank
you, no further conversation needed just thank you, these are the only
words you seem worthy of so thank you. The other words are and never
will be reflective of something coming out of my mouth to touch and
destroy your core for that's not me, I would never to step off that cliff of
depths unknown for you have shown me not how to treat maybe how to
beat someone into subjection with words of desperation, creating a
sense of security for yourself when nothing is secure, not even your feet
planted evenly on the ground, with a push you quickly lose your balance
and off track you go as you have taken me but recovery soon takes hold
creating that sound firm foundation that Momma used to talk about,
that solid foundation that Granny used to sing about, so thank you for
knocking me off course to a better course a more solid foundation to
stand on my own.

Mind's Eye Thoughts...

I never gave you control, I simply granted you access, not to come inside reprogram the system (me) but to see how it functions, not to create a malfunction in that junction box I call my head. The card you were given was all access granted but you took for granted a privilege not often given and you gave all you had with all the tools at your disposal, but to your dismay and watch your mind decay while reading another proposal that was written way before your presence was realized. I had already been talked about and overly criticized, so I surmised a plan to malfunction proof my mind, intertwine with all the thoughts of sabotage. You grow more persistent for the combination you know not, you have what you have, I got what is not. Not respect, more neglect, more of dejection but my deflection of your words has turned the tables as it seems, no more restless nights or cold sweat dreams.

Let Go

I don't want to let you go but if you must go, go in silence not saying a word, no explanation needed all boundaries have been exceeded to points of no return. Go now my love, look back no more, close the door, roll up the window, put the gas pedal to the floor. My thoughts have always been to have you near and dear for as long as you allowed, now my presence no longer wanted nor is it allowed. I don't want to let you go but if I must I will, all the time spent, emotions laid out, you told me you were here as long as I wanted, needed, desired you but something changed, rearranged words to mean nothing more than just syllables brought together to form what you call words of the heart, from the heart, when in reality they just rolled off your tongue from no other place than the deepest part of your throat but you gloat about heartfelt, yeah I feel your heartbeat as if on the surface, yes your words are surface proof not being able to penetrate no further than the surface of my skin. Regression, suppression trying to run from the fact that you have not only touched my heart you have scratched my soul leaving a mark, your stamp of everlasting emotion, swimming in an ocean of confusion giving an illusion of moments of happiness. I don't want to let you go but if I must I will for I have never been one to hold one with chains. I have never been one to bar one from life or the life they want to lead. I have never been one to hold one from expansion of mind and body, both sculpted to make a better us but trust being the main ingredient to form this masterpiece. I have never been one to hold one back from true happiness, my definition may be too far distant from yours not being able to meet in the middle, too much to shuffle, too many moving parts, not enough time to create that intended bond. I don't want to let you go but if I must I will, just come back ...

Paradise (SG3)

Ever wonder why the best of times seem to close and run short of time but really they haven't, it's simply delayed until the next time. Have you ever been put in a place so perfectly placed that like minds seem like one mind, one thought when all think so differently. If conversations could break ground it would have built a structure built for the Kings we are. Each room flawlessly placed to reflect the gift of life and the breathes taken are released for relaxation of mind body and soul haven' taken on a whole new meaning. The libations flow like waterfalls, cooling and heating the soul to reflect the sun's rays as it beams down and warms the waters below and find me in tow as well as it pulls you under not to drown but to breathe.

Life changes

As I look back over this short thing I call life, I reflect on times past that have transcended above all comprehension and understanding, sometimes overwhelming sometimes too demanding. Some of my years seem to elude me and continue to hide from my memory, dense fog and clouds of darkness intensify as light tries to come through. My childhood as I refer to my manhood has created this person you see now standing sometimes on hollow ground, shaky legs just barely holding on to hopes of a better tomorrow for sorrow has once again stepped into place and taken hold of another piece of my heart. The experience of life has taught me that death is all but normal in my eyes; the cries are just another way for me to empty out my soul only to be filled once more with more tears and fears of losing someone else. My life has taught me to value one's present, value the ones that exist, value the hug, value the kiss, and value the wish for a better day coming. My days so often reflect on my past to develop and move forward to the future and making sure the present is filled with nothing but good times for times change in the blinking of an eye and the cries start again, and as with all men I too have my days, my nights when I ponder and wonder about what ifs, the what could have been if they were still here. How would I act, how would I react to seeing them again ... could I hold back my tears of joy or would I be filled with rage and say why did you leave me all alone to weather this storm called life. Words spoke would be said ... "you have done well my son, you have done all expected you would, you have made ways for yourself and others, you have supported family and friends and especially your brothers.

I know my time seemed short, when things were looking up so much, but I had to go and leave and never to return but I'm here whenever you need, I have watched you daily on your journey, whether you fail or succeed." Those are the words I hear daily when I think of all the times we shared, glad I had a friend like that, our conversations never left a stone unturned, encouragement never ceased but your face I can no longer touch, your hair I can no longer run my fingers through as I grease your scalp as you sit on the floor, my core bruised but remains in tack. Your ways have become mine, my nasty disposition you would always speak of still shows its ugly head every now again but again that's who I am, you accepted me for being just me, now all others will also. You showed me how to treat a woman, some of the experiences taught me what I would tolerate nor generate harm towards another woman. I think about my past and link it to my future for you have molded, scolded and shouldered all my transgressions. I often think about the story told of your beautiful yellow dress on that warm November day, your weight loss program all signs of great success, they talked about your walk and all the control displayed, not knowing that night you were called with no interruption, no let me finish this, no let me finish that, you were gone in an instant and instantly life changed for me.

Lose control

Lose control to gain control of your body with mine attached as a feeling of being complete. Lose control to lose your mind for the moment and come back to reality and realize that climax had been reached, surpassed in your mind still focused on the moment, never losing eye contact, our bodies stay connected fused together as melted steel. Lose control as I admire every aspect of you from the top of your head to the balls of your feet, to what's inside your head to what's deep down in your heart. lose control and let down the gates of reservation, let me temp all your temptations, making thoughts reality, dreams come true for it's you I crave, it's you I so much want to consume when consumption is not an option. I want to be able to look at you from a distance and your knees start to shake, not from nervousness but my eyes being felt undressing you, my hands all over your body, my tongue, well the picture so vivid in your mind no need to go further, just come to me.

Read A little deeper

Expressions of love, heartfelt pain for things we have no control over, but emotional attachments have taken on a whole new meaning, defining our paths as one, one without the other is loneliness of mind and bodies not being connected. Where is your heart really, do I hold a piece or part, mine has come to rest in yours? Where is your heart really, do I have a firm hold on it, or is it just temporarily placed next to mine to be removed not by my own hands but the hands of a stranger to me, you not so much, although foreign to me, a familiar touch to you. I read a little deeper into my own thoughts, my fears become apparent as my reality sits right in front of me, whispering sweet nothings in my ear, "you love her more than you know, you have gone farther than you thought you would go, love is not a switch you turn off and on ... " I realize that, and my future hurt is overshadowed by the present feeling of happiness fulfilled daily with expressions of trueness as we see it. I will continue to push forward the present, not allowing that future hurt ever to take hold, but hold on I'm coming. Arrival made, destination not known, no departure even thought of, here to stay, my heart and all.

Effortless

Being remise to dismiss the level of effort needed to love you, I'm reminded of a time long ago as a child running wild with no worries, just curiosity to uncover the mysteries of the day. I step back to stand above and look down upon your beauty as it shines as rays of light being taken from the sun to give back to the moon. Effortless beauty, effortless joy you have bestowed upon me, never wanting to look back nor look forward but stay right here in this moment, this point and time, realizing time never stops but slows for our enjoyment. The adornment of your body as it releases energy never felt before, as it gives it also takes and holds near all the love I care to give but forgive my effortless flow of speech as I reach into your soul to grab hold and never let go. No stronghold but a gentle caress of your flesh as it melts in my hands as shea butter from the warmness, hands never needing to rub together for you give off more heat and the passion never stops following. Effortlessly you have granted me parts of you no one has ever witnessed, but effortlessly, I also grant that same right and right here I will be without effort.

Foundation

I drop my bags to establish and build a new foundation, one built with all the needed and necessary materials. Trust was added to help withstand the load of misguided judgment and faulty thoughts. Love poured in as rebar reinforcement so it never breaks, nor cracks with the passing of time; being able to stand tall and not bend against the hardest of blows from this thing we call life. Loyalty the corner pieces that help to evenly distribute the weight of daily temptation. Faith is firmly established over all of structure, holding all parts together. A New house is the structure; the new home is in the heart with both being simultaneously erected, even in the midst of a storm. No old baggage allowed for all things are new, no furniture needed for this will be new too. A house may be empty but a home is fully furnished with love, trust, respect and loyalty all constructed of material not made by man but graciously given to us from above.

Clear Thoughts...

Can I step back and away and still be close to you but more of a physical sense leaving my emotions and my heart at the door only linking to them not in your presence but with your absence as I find peace and with you I can release all the pressure of the day and let it flow on you and put a glow on you. Not saying there is no longer a connection for my erection will last longer than the most interesting conversation you've ever had. With no questions asked to find out who I am and where I came from, I can't relate to my life as a lie so I keep that only for the one truly interested for I hear myself speaking empty words of admiration and the generation of lust, forget about the trust as it's too far gone to ever come back so we connect to reconnect only our body parts for they are the ones that matter most right. All giving way to detached emotion as we swim in a sea of bliss with a gentle kiss to let you know I'm here when actually I'm alone in my mind as it wrestles with the expression of nonverbal communication being transmitted through my fingertips as I lay hands to caress every part of your exterior, not even wanting to see the interior for if it's hollow, I can't pour all of me out so to have nothing left but an empty shell called me.

Through The Eyes of the Soul

I almost ....

I almost lost my mind trying to find what didn't want to be found as the sound of my own voice started to crack from lack of substance and the subject matter no longer made sense so why was I trying to make sense of a nonsense situation, shaking my head because I almost did.

I almost let my dreams become reminiscent thoughts as I tried to look and ask for answers to a problem that would have long been solved if I had used the resolve and evolved into the man I supposed, am and will always be. Now my dreams are reality and no longer a fallacy because I almost let my
chance slip away.

I was about to let my team orientated spirit be taken for granted and be left on the field by myself to win the impossible as I almost didn't take that timeout to regroup and discover my inner beast as I released the skill of many men being only one and conquer I did but I almost didn't.

I virtually went virtual seeking likes as if they paid bills, and thrills were short lived since I don't post drama or ask for help with my inner peace for peace of mind helped change my mind because I almost lost it.

I almost told a story about life and how perception can lead to deception, as wise tales become life tales hoping someone would hear it. I still got a story to tell but I almost told it.

I almost looked to someone else to redeem me when I was reminded that I am my own redemption for someone else may add clauses to an already voided contract so I almost didn't cash in my redemption.

I almost let my expressiveness become a thing of the past but that wasn't and still isn't me, just as I express my heart, I can at the same time beat on my chest just like the rest and let my nonverbal communication be sign language to the blind, non-existent but I will forever exist with my expressiveness or else I'll go silent.

Thinking OuT LOUD!

Do thoughts cross your mind that you want to say out loud but can't, but why can't you they are yours, they are genuine, they are your truth, they are coming from a reliable source, yourself. How can ones' perception of self be determined by likes from ones you don't even know.

How can attraction be lost, but suddenly found when the one you lost interest in has attracted someone else?

How can time be so valuable but you waste it on people and things that don't matter?

As I was asked just the other day do you know so and so? "No I don't", well they are your Facebook friend. "Well I still don't know this person, as a matter of fact, if my life depended on me picking them out of a lineup, I would be dead, and with that said I hope you get the idea that I don't know them. I'm sure this story resonates with some, not all, but for the most part it's part of the social media generation.

Through The Eyes of the Soul

Insecurity Scattered

Not wanting to lose you confuses me with thoughts of insecurity but actions always prove assurances true. The thought of losing you makes my mind ponder in places of no return but you always throw me a lifeline to pull me back and hold me even tighter. Deception crosses my mind soon perception follows closely behind wiping all doubt that may linger. I can't put my finger on you as you move to fast, your words I take to heart and your actions make them last. I wonder would you leave me for him when I left her, leaving me standing alone separated from who I once was, then the buzz starts of what I had, what I lost and what I lost again. To bend over backwards, making sacrifices only to find out in the end it was all in vain, all just a game. What a relief it is to be used by you, those were my thoughts before growth took hold to show me a woman of character, a woman with qualities not too often seen, I mean you are amazing. Yes, my thinking a cluster fuck, a disaster waiting to take form. When you make plans you always say we and not just you, you include me in every aspect of your life never leaving me to wonder if I was ever given a chance. Does your love for me lose its luster, only to be transformed into something not known, hardly shown and barely hanging on? The love I have for you a seed planted, a root formed, out of the ground it comes for the world to see its beauty, a display of honesty, openness, tenderness, laughter and joy. Days filled with kisses, nights filled with love making leaving no space in between for any type of confusion or the creation of an illusion for what you see is real and consistently duplicating my love for you becomes second nature and a part of me so to lose you I would be losing a part of me.

I've considered my ways as paths often traveled by other men but none stay on the road too long so the pavement becomes smoother as a road less traveled, many side streets to pull off and start a new journey but me I stay the course chosen until I'm told or otherwise feel I need to head in another direction. I try to stay focused on the positive as negative leads to thinking not so creative. I sometimes make assumptions my truth often not looking at the circumstances surrounding my thoughts, assumptions are my truth or not always the truth but false visuals in my mind. Confidence is a quality taught as I go back in time to recreate already given facts about you.

———————————————————————

Love Me Thoughts...

Here I find myself in a place I have never been before, dazed and confused, used and not cognizant of what's going on around me but everyone else does. I wake to a flurry of blows from the past, present and future not knowing how to respond but all of a sudden life dawned on me for it was the true teacher. I refused to listen, I refuse to see the signs as they were posted so eloquently along the way, stop, listen, don't go there, don't do this, don't do that, yet and still I ignored and soared to heights that were no taller than I. I grasped for straws only to come up with toothpicks, no use for me at this point as its air I need to breathe and find a place of understanding. I jump through hoops only to nets that have been removed so I feel the ridges and nothing to sooth my pass through. If I'm like other men I hope they take heed and not let bleed out all that has been taken from me, I think I have left me to find a place of nonexistence, a wonderer looking for something that's out there but even if I found it I would not know the difference because I'm different and no longer the same as before. Confidence shattered, manhood battered, I'm no good for anyone, that's why I left myself. I'm gone ...

Addiction

If my addiction was you, would you recommend rehab to clear thoughts of a fairytale love and an endless vibe of tranquility?
If my addiction was you, do I lose my ability to reach back and touch me for my hands are filled with you?
If my addiction was you, what drug would you recommend I digest to regress from considering you my backbone, my go hard or go home, my ride or die, or do I let my heart pulsate in your hands, listen to the beat as it plays tunes saying "Call My Name",
can you hear it, most importantly can you feel it. Yes I have chosen you my drug of choice, no remorse as I rejoice with visions of you in my mind, distance could never separate me from my addiction as it's an affliction I chose to bear, but my addiction, you misperceived as a hindrance and a closure of space, you can't even recognize that you are my drug of choice, my addiction, my affliction. You are my habit hard to break but with your refusal to accept, I have no other choice but to go through this shit called withdrawal.

Mars Men Women Venus

Discussion being based on understanding not demanding that Mars comes to Venus which is impossible when we think about scientific reasoning, but with reasoning being a factor to understanding, do we seek that? Venus being the larger force similar to the earth, its variations are close to the represented force of our residence, but evidence proves it's still not the earth, similarly Mars smaller in size has its complexities making it even more intriguing from a distance but close up a simple planet with limited understanding. Justification not needed for either existence just understanding of their existence and presence.

Further discussion illuminates' differences often not thought about but heard, often not talked about but seen. Men being Mars, smaller in internal structure but larger in size have many more dynamics than scientifically proven, no we are not closer to the Sun as we burn easily, just as your words strike the core of our being, but our resilience keeps us from displaying any weakness as the canyons once thought of to hold water but are just wounds that refuse to heal, but you still think we don't feel the simplest of words coming from a planet so close and appeared so similar. Venus being the women, the hottest prancing about the earth and Mars representative of the man his temperatures only reaching a little above some of the coldest felt in the south.

Men like Mars don't heat up unless the temperatures right, and women being from Venus stay hot, stay ready, stay in the moment but men of Mars have long since evolved, old canals as wounds and volcanoes that no longer erupt but go through the motions until the sun rotates close enough to heat us up, but these moments still exist and show their presence sometimes in moments that you are wanted in the moment but the movement of the stars has not just aligned so be mindful as we are aware it's not too appealing dealing with a mind so delusional but pivotal moments occur when fact meets fiction and

Fantasy becomes reality as we make dreams come true and those volcanoes that remain dormant start to erupt with emotion and those canals that were so deep start to fill with the love that you so unconditionally give and we start to live in the moment just as you.

But that moment seems to be defined as the future for you as you look pass my presence and look to my past to try to determine where we are. We are right here, right now and only if you would let that be as it may and stay in the moment and if you could fast forward the moment you will see we are still right here, where we were, loving and vibing, creating moments as if it were just yesterday when we locked eye contact and you saw me and I saw you as being the hottest thing walking, the smoothest thing talking. Just vibe with me, just enjoy the moment called life as we rotate around the earth together.

Reflection!

I see you for who you are even when you look into my eyes and see darkness a black canvass with shadows looming in the background. I see you for who you are even if the winds take a turn and dust is thrown like layers of mud from swamp land in bayou. I see you as you are even when doubt sneaks in to cause havoc in my mind and my thoughts and actions become one fighting against each other to dominate the other. I saw you for who you are when I first laid eyes on your smile some time ago and I look back and still see the same one I saw then, I see you regardless of my actions and words because they sometimes cause havoc in my mind and if you don't mind as I lay my head down to rest for my inner turmoil has caused havoc on my mind as I think the worse and since I have killed my good thoughts first and the only ones that remain are the ones that drive me insane and they remain close to me as if they were my best friend to remind me that what you see and what you hear are nothing less than fairy tale lies not cries but screams of destruction but as always daybreak raises creating and eruption of the truth to who you really are, I can't help but see and feel the boiling over lava from yourself feed up with negative connotations, accusations to a reputation that has never been tarnished but well-polished as the world sees your shine so why can't I, I keep telling you my thoughts and actions are causing havoc in my mind to fight to remain but I'll continue to fight and break these chains of relentless torture to my own mind because I know who you were and who you are.

Through The Eyes of the Soul

The Devil in Disguise

When I first saw her, I didn't even know she was staring at me. She initially just glanced my way as I glanced back at her from across the room. Eye contact made on a couple of occasions but no advances on either part. So as time passed and the sightings more often, I felt I was getting to know her from a distance as I watched her make her way around the room only having brief meaningless conversations with men and women. So my observations grew to curiosity wanting to find out who this mystery woman was. Never seeing her with anyone but being with everyone, she was the life of the party creating levels of confusion only in a dream.

My shyness would not let me approach her the way I wanted so I just waited, but it seems she read my mind and started to approach me but not in the obvious manner. She walked passed me brushing ever so lightly against me so I felt the softness of her touch. She would walk by just to say excuse me putting her hand in the middle of my back as if holding me up to keep me from falling. If I were standing or sitting at the bar she would come over and bend over the bar making her cleavage visual to the naked eye and that fragrance it was breathe taking, not too much just enough to get on the hairs of my nose and stay there until the next time I saw her.

After working on my own confidence to approach her with the right words and all the time words were never needed to be said it was already understood the connection we made was already in full effect. Nonverbal communication was something I was not used to but I figure I could get with this program because it was something about this woman that had my mind in a supernatural state. As time went on the attraction grew to addiction and soon to be understood was a lesson to be learned. She in all her cunning manipulated my mind to a point of no return, making all my wrongs seem right and right was a thing of the past.

She begins to torment my soul to depths only reached in points of constant meditation and concentration. She tore out my heart so many times I became heartless and could not feel my own heart beat for she had it in her hands and my life was slowly but surely becoming engulfed in her. She even tried to break through my character, my foundation for existing to disable and reprogram my thinking but something powerful happened and life started to revert back to where I once was, I started to get me back but I knew she would not go down without a fight and even after I got rid of her she still tries to come visit every now and again but all can say is I'm thankful to her and for her showing her true colors as I would have never guessed her real name was Jealousy.

Confused Thoughts...

So often I've wondered about the distance but my persistence has met
its match not giving one inch but in a pinch if found I'm right there but
for how long tho. But for how long tho do you keep putting your mind
in places it no longer belongs. Some signs have been obvious and others
not so outright but they are right where they need to be for you can't
even climb stairs when it was once the norm, you are contained and
constrained to one room thinking you may bring gloom or throw shade
even when blinds were never opened. Constant blows of accusations
made, but I thought my retributions had been paid with the lockout
once before of a wide open door. Even with the physical door being
open the mental one is closed off to me but I see where it is open but
it's not for me and like you said there will never be three included in the
equation so minus one bringing me down to zero where I once had
value but none no more so why don't I care less and make you faceless
in my eyes as someone I once knew but try to recollect the events of
past, at the ones that brought smiles for miles of beach, still have to be
explored but now ignored to continue this journey all alone at least that's
the appearance that wants to be given but actions paint a more chilling
adventure. How is it that one will allow one to continue to bend and
give reason when that one knows that the season has ended some time
ago but slow to release the pain thinking this will lessen the strain for
that brain has already overcome so much but your touch was all that was
needed but you seceded from the union cutting all connections to your
own island but one still tries to reach the unreachable.

So will it ever be realized that a love was had and lust was left behind
because of its shelf life, a decision was made to throw infatuation to side
due to its shelf life being even shorter, but trueness of love once known
even tho grown you saw it, you felt it but sadly you didn't want it for the
season had expired and a hired hand had arrived to clean up the
residue leaving no parts of me to remain as now it's not the same and no
it's not a game of cat and mouse or maybe playing house on the inside
but outside presenting clues to the clueless but they know just as I know.

They are glad for you and at the same time sad for you, telling you to come outside and let the world see the love in your eyes for they see it up close but it looks so much better from a distance at that time my persistence will become nonexistent. How can I be mystified or terrified by this feeling of what may be perceived as temporary moments of insanity? Being so insanely encompassed in your world that my world has lost its reason to exist but I persist to keep that gate open for closure would be closure of mind and body. These two factions have been joined at the hip since the beginning of time and time has shown that no matter how separated the two may seem they are one. I come to you with open arms and a closed off heart so I thought but once again you have caught me in your snares of pleasure, a place of pure bliss, a kiss like no other, a lover never to compare and where can I find another like you if I lose you can you advise or at least compromise on your secrets that have engulfed me like a tornado in the midst of fiery skies and devastating winds.

How can I be so nonobservant and not observe my reflection in the mirror, reflecting back on rays of momentous light as a star studded sky clear as the day. How can I or do I even bother to reconstruct my smile to make it anything other than what it is, even in time of complete frustration with self, I ask self to prove things other than what's shown but moans of resistance not persistence to change what has already been constructed. At the end of the day I lay my head against yours to gain a better perspective at a vision of truth.

You Did Tell Me!

Why wouldn't I listen when you were painting that vision that you had moved on. So scorned from the words that I missed the conversation had that ended it all and started a new beginning with me nowhere in sight but with sleight of hand you put me back in your space without my permission as if your mission was to cloud my vision which had become clear. You put your hands back on me and not in an abusive sense but I sensed that you wanted me back but it was only temporary as I have become secondary and my primary function is to give you what you want provide you with what you need at the time for its only temporary as I am now secondary but can't prove it so I move my position back without your permission and my vision becomes blurred once again and I put myself in the ranks of some other men waiting in line for the chance to romance you, impress you, undress you only to be Mind fucked by you. Glad I know better, glad I went back and read that letter my mother wrote me years ago to tell me, I'm more than what you perceive me to be, I'm more than rejection of an erection because you've already had your fill. I'm more than secondary, I'm more than temporary because I need and will always want to be
primary so I marry myself.

Does she still exist?

You know that one with some old school ways and a whole lot of new school flavor, the one with whom the conversation is always on point and the take away you savor. One whose ways reflect more of things of the past than what she had in past to bring it to the present making for a not so certain future at least for some because I wonder does she still exist. One whose virtues are never tainted by what the world does or sees as a trend, she is one of true integrity and her standards will not be broken, regardless of the outer appearance for nothing she will bend. One whose words are always with kindness, nothing never said to kill the spirit, only up building and reassurance giving insurance that this triple A policy will never expire but grow in its value with the highest return possible because for this small investment I promise to make all your dreams come true even the ones not even thought of whether big or small but I still wonder does she still exist? No fuck yous maybe I want to suck you, as we give in kind satisfaction with the reaction always being one of pleasure never having to think about the measure of time spent for a moment can last forever so time limits don't exist even if it's just a kiss to say hello and good bye is never spoken of more like see you later so good bye is never going to be better for goodbye is forever even spoken of in a letter.

Truth is a choice

What is truth really? Is it a manifestation of one's thoughts as you
perceive reality to be? Is truth really the truth when it's told in parts and
not it's totality, when the total is found and put all together what would
be lost beside the respect from one to another, does it mean that much
to lose that which you thought you had waiting patiently in the
background hoping they would never see you for who you really are.
The truth slides only half way across your lips but you say it's a choice
when the truth has always been whole and anything otherwise is a lie,
guess we're all liars creating fires of deception and you really thought the
reception was going to be one of gratitude when your attitude and
actions spoke something else. Let's be real, let's tell the truth because
life without truth always leads down a road to destruction one way or
another. Choices are made for the betterment of one's self but not at the
expense of someone else, who else deserves the choice of truth over the
choice to blur lines when all the time the story had already been written.
Those same choices when you ask someone else to make, need to be
more concrete with little substance other than the truth, no deception
sprinkled within just the truth no matter how salty it taste, so why can't I
have the same flavor. What can be said when words create a void like
no other, why bother to express your thoughts when they go from here
to there with no destination in Mind on to find they have been
discarded like trash removed. How do you recover when cover is
nonexistent and the rain continues to fall and coldness starts to
overcome the air? What else can be said, what else can be done when a
made up Mind has received it's so called calling but whispers still find
their way in the shadows.

What is one to do when confusion is the only option, and thoughts reflect the same but hope renders grace and mercy to say it will be ok? A mind in turmoil is like a piece of wood being put through a grinder only to find wood chips to be scattered here and there and everywhere but how can you provide solitude when your attitude is so different from before, opening up your heart now all of a sudden closing the door. Amazing you are, and amazing you will continue to be but trying to keep you close is too much for me so I love you enough to let you go. I refuse to let my spirit be tortured with the pain thrown this way.

A Couple of Forever's are Not Needed

Fast forward to forever and tomorrow will cease to exist as the urge to be anxious about the next day will fade, for all days will be filled with unforgettable moments, even if nothing is the agenda - we are. No cares. For the world is our platter, as we scatter us in every corner only to come back and see we're still there. We are the sand on beaches as they reach shore-to-shore and the more you spread it out, it still finds a way of coming back together, because we do have forever, and as clever as it seems, the lever called reality has been broken and the token of love that we grant each other has paid in advance a couple of forever's when one is only needed. Our lives filled with a never-ending flow of possibilities and the responsibilities are all to us, as we thrust ourselves overboard to swim in the ocean of each other's mind for they have become interwoven to make one, and burnt on both ends creating an inseparable bond, that forever is not enough time to separate.

Silent Night

As the sun passes its midpoint and the day comes to a close, the temperature starts to fall and now a chill has come over me. Let us break out the blankets to sit in front a slow burning; the nights just begun no time soon should we tire. Your eyes reflect the flames, and your body glistens from the oils applied shortly before, I kiss you with tenderness trying to reach your core. The core of your being where you let all cares be the past, and the present moment, let's stay here and make it last. Let us make love together with our souls bonded as one, let us make love without sound for your expression will be volume enough. I will hear your screams, your moans as tones of joy and pleasure and will go silently into the good night, hold each other all through the night as will not be a factor for our love force will stop time in its tracks so we can let our minds run free, from and to each other. We can be silent yet still understood, as our minds will have conversations of the what ifs but we stay in the moment. I want something warm, I want something sweet, and I want to take my time with this one, slow and deep.

Fuck all the BS I Gotta GO!

One eye closes as the other tries to focus on something in the not so far distant. Pain starts to overcome all of my mental facilities making it impossible to imagine the implausible coming to existence but resistance helps me to fight a little longer even though stronger I am not becoming but a numbing of my interior and my exterior has already presented my plight and at this time, on this night I can no longer fight the good fight for it had been fought and I have sought out peace not in man but in he who brought me forth and now takes me back to where I originated and so beautifully created in an image not even a mirror could replicate as I dedicate my life back to him. I say thank you.

Before ...

I often wondered if I put that smile on your face as I erased all thoughts of a fallacy of someone who was never going to be mine, just tried to make a conscious effort to keep you close, when you've always been so far from my truth as my roots remain true and that glue that kept us within eye view soon lost its sticking power as the last hour arrived trying to bring life to a non-responsive corpse. Before reluctance was resistance to post any relative connections to the life I lived, giving life to control as I scrolled down a timeline of deception wanting to keep a good name for the people as if they really cared, for they stared at the situation as one all too familiar hoping and praying that eyes would open before being swallowed up by a fallacy where jealousy existed for a reason as treason was committed in front of the all-seeing eyes except mine. Now you are speaking French where English is the primary language realizing that the secondary responses are affirmation as the temptation to respond has fleeted from me for best wishes are in order as my steps will forever walk a different path never crossing again. Now a friendship status is more of a connection that will never spark again as any glimmer of hope has expired for time and distance gives life to a once dead situation. Best of life to all involved for I have evolved and *see* the revolving door continues to open and close even when denial of relations makes for a mystery solved three times over as you start over and over just as before. Now I bid you goodbye not as before. Long walks in the park in the dark trying to find my inner strength, trying to make sense of all the convoluted information floating about my brain. Insane I'm not, crazy I will never be, but find myself having crazy thoughts, with fears of rejection and making no exceptions to myself for myself because I'm not the rule that was set but I tried to abide by them but in their sly way tried to undermine what I thought was something beautiful no it was cute.

Extension of Goodness

Reaching heights taller than the highest building, your emotions will be added lubrication as you go on this vacation with me. This extension of goodness opens you up, easing your tension so you can view love making from another dimension. Let yourself be free as this extension of goodness fills even the deepest void for your walls massage this goodness with goodness. Your hips move as if Caribbean blood flowed through your veins leading to your safe place as I erase any thought of your past and the last thought you will ever have is me and this extension of me for we come together but leave separated for my mind is with you and still wanting to be inside you as you release your juices that were once so elusive but the conclusion had been reached just as your climax since the max of my extension is headed in every direction creating a mold of me for acceptance of me for your body will reject any other foreign objects and my objection is not even warranted. Your mind becomes mine for they are intertwined and the rewind button is the only one that exist as we find something new and exciting each and every time for no second is wasted. Where did y'all come from are words often stated for no one has ever given me satisfaction and a consistency guarantee that has no expiration date only one of fine wine that with the passing of time gets better, only that you can refill your glass as many times as your heart desires and a reservation is never required. My goodness is extended to you with unconditional love for my rising up is a laying down of you naked exposed as I caress the stress from every limb and limp you are until my extension of goodness awakens your nerve endings as pain of entry is the precursor to pleasure only experienced in a dream. I embrace you from all angles as you take my mind with every stroke, you scream I moan, I hold and you try so hard to let go, not of me but this feeling that's been aroused for miles can't reduce this feeling. This moment I touch you my extension and not to mention my heart beat becomes one with yours. I can't get you out of my head or off my head as they have become one and separation at this moment is not an option. Tbc

5.4.3.2.1

5.4.3.2. 1... gives choice another chance to thrive and survive to see another day for time cannot be recovered, kind of like if we had discovered this or that sooner we would have made better choices, probably not, as some invoices have to be paid on delivery and others up front, kind of like buying a new car as if it's ours, no title in hand just a payment book to reflect with each payment you are that much closer to it being yours or is it. 5 4 3 2 1 ... here comes choice again trying to be chosen and I've already made my mind up with little to no regard for anyone or anything, only this immediate gratification which leads to temporary satisfaction and a reaction that reflects true choice for 5 4 3 2 1... was used as a buffer for decisions made.

Part II

The Eyes

..... .I see things thru eyes of no regret only choices we make, circumstances may dictate consequences but duplication sometimes makes it easier to deal; but the feelings become stronger, the yearning becomes deeper, the distance brings you closer, to what?

Through The Eyes of the Soul

Is there another!

One that possesses the qualities that are so expressive that expression gives vision to the blind, gives light to the darkest soul for no control is needed just me. That one conversationalist that makes your interest the topic of conversation for evening and small talk doesn't have a chance, it's not romance just a glance at what it looks like for you to be someone's undivided attention. Despite the noise despite the chatter, your voice is the only one that matters, the only one being heard. One that looks beyond your smile to see the storm brewing within you and be willing to be your hiding place from the storm resting in his arms being held just tight enough for your breath to meet his due to closeness. Is there another that will shed tears and take your cares as his own and still own his own truth when a lie could have fit the mold as well. One that could give more than a couple of forever's but willing to make the most of the moment to see where it leads with the only guidance being two souls connected through vides of wholeness and realness not even being an option. Is there another that can intoxicate your mind with endless flows of conversation so mind blowing that the bedroom is the afterthought for your body has already been satisfied?

TBC

———————————————

Believe In Me

Even If you have to tell me a lie to help me find my truth for your belief is my release as all other opinions cease to exist. Fake believe that I'm your superhero and I'll show you a world full of endless possibilities as tranquility and peace fall on our shoulders as feathers just gently tickling out passions for we're no longer rationing out the belief in the other. They say fake it until you make it, why can't you fake your belief in Me until you start to believe in Me and all of a sudden you see it. You can touch it because you believed in Me, I found me to find us and the trust that was diminished has been replenished as you relinquished control of your positive thoughts and let them flow on me like a waterfall for every breath I took was deeper than the last as I grasp hold of this journey called life and brought forth my truth and presented it to you as a sacrifice of sorts not for you to throw darts at creating holes for my dreams to dissipate and never appear again. So I begin to take my thoughts, my fears, my cares, my heart back to me because I started to believe in myself.

My Eyes

My Eyes have seen the depths of a soul dug out to be scattered in a field as discarded trash and the vast majority sit and watch to see who and what will pick up the pieces.

My eyes have witnessed life almost sacrificed as the screams from my voice gave an escape route to life only to be taken in the blinking of an eye for my cries went unheard and the louder I got the quieter it became as I heard my own echoes as music playing to a different beat, my defeat for my eyes had seen dreams turn to nightmares, once heart felt hugs became what the fuck stares.

My eyes have seen a relationship transform from love to dam near hate at a rate that only compares to NASCAR and no speedy recovery was nowhere in sight for demise had been planned and the demands to compromise became greater, you better act now, don't wait to later for each night closed not with a smile but with bewildered and weary eyes because the days had become longer and emotions stronger for a fallacy bound for failure from the start as it caused demise before my eyes to life as I knew it.

My eyes have seen the transformation of a mind never twisted but I see listed a list of choices and the voices spoke a language called Hennessey and bend you see I did, and on a slippery slope I slide into a world of hopes and dreams more like terror and screams but at the time my eyes could not see but my eyes have seen. My eyes have witnessed a love so deep that comprehension of that dimension is like an out of body experience. How can someone love so hard and let go so easily and on return hold on so tightly.

My eyes have seen that my life is unique to a degree at the same time the same as so many before me, with me and so to be after me.

Through The Eyes of the Soul

My eyes at times have been closed and swollen shut from tears of joy
knowing the pain no longer persist and yet I resist the thought that this
person is gone and no longer here, no longer in my eyesight, only when
I close my eyes do I see them, only when I close my eyes I feel them,
only when I close my eyes I smell them, so I scream from within why
can't I see them.

My eyes have seen my own body transform from words of motivation
perceived as defamation. Do you see all the work I've done, no let me
show you, look at this creation?

How long will it last and how long could I live in
the past because it became the past the moment after it parted from
your lips but I kept reliving the past as if it were the present that
prevented me from being in the present, so all you ever experienced
was the past.

<u>Does it ...</u>

Does the wheel stop turning because you have put on the brakes,
giving others double takes when they shouldn't have even gotten a
first glance? Do connections ever reconnect if they are both burnt on
both ends or do they trim back the edges to expose the new, whether
a new you, new chapter regardless its new and who knew you could
reconnect with passion and not have to ration it out but let it flow as
electricity through your veins for it slows for no one, full force all the
time, even when the breaker blows it's still there. Does love stop
manifesting itself in us or do we stop love from manifesting and start
investing in Penny stocks hoping for huge returns when the most we
can get is minimal at best and yet we still believe people harbor the
best for us while the rest of just act as onlookers only slowing to see
if its devastation so we can collect the details to report back.

T.D.

Emotional Thoughts...

How can truth and reality be so far apart that deception and confusion appear to be normal? How can what you hear and what you see go hand and hand but your hands can't even come together to applaud the visual given and the grace received. How can ones' dreams become nightmares when at one time it was a fairy tale of fallacy glazed over with mind blowing tactics even the military couldn't comprehend? How can a once calm demeanor be transformed into one that's God's gift to the world and the only one that's aware of the promotion and the notion to think that all should bow down as if a clown show had commenced and convinced even the most mindful that this was a true picture not knowing all the time it was fiction and a benediction of what was.

Time ...

What is time?
Is time a reflection of your past giving you time to reflect and redirect
your energy somewhere else or is more time to reminisce thinking
about that first kiss that will never happen again or is it the spin you put
on it in your mind to remind you of all that once was. There was once a
time when Santa existed but we all grew up to realize that he
represented gifts that ultimately represented bills to one's that
appreciation became expectation of the one making dreams come true
on a thought of kindness but the blindness of selfishness seeped in and
created a facade and you remembered what I didn't get you compared
to what I did so time stood still. Time never gives us a blank slate to
start over with, just a slate to mark on for the mistakes made and the
grade at the end is if we have room remaining. Are you gaining time by
changing the time on your watch as daylight savings time gives one hour
and takes the other refuge to give back a few months later as a perceived
gift of additional light at the end of a nonexistent tunnel, for I'm sleep
deprived already. But steady the course for remorse is time stood still
and I gift back that hour that was given to me as a time of reflection
because the moonlight consoles and sunlight stirs up, so I choose the
latter for the darkness reflects my meditation not as medication but as
realness for the sunlight should never be apparent more than the parent
as they equally shine.

Now I'm a friend ...

So much history, now I'm a friend. You say we're starting over but it seems that it's over and too far gone to recover especially since I was your lover at one time but now I'm a friend. Kind of like getting way deep with someone, knowing their deepest and darkest but all of a sudden telling them let's ignore what was and let's focus on the surface, superficial things, fake emotions and whatever else that has no real relevance. It's understood you want to be in charge this time setting the tone and making the calls but where does the man reside and what decisions can I make if any since you are the one writing the story, so it's your glory not mine because now I'm a friend. I understand you being my best friend, being able to communicate on any and all levels but not allowing yourself to feel and feel me because you want to be the one holding the pen to say when it starts and when it's ends. As of late my mind has been at ease, my souls at peace as I can finally feel the breeze and breathe fresh air. You've put your boundaries in place and based on what's been seen no thought of me crossing at any point and you constantly point out the difference. When my own are established what will be your reaction, will our friendship grow or continue to lose traction. So things I now chose to believe because the truth would destroy our friendship or any hope for a relationship and ripe my heart right out of my chest taking my last breath away but now I'm a friend so what does it matter if at all.

Wild Thoughts...

I can feel you cummin' as your leg muscles tighten, your head starting to jerk, I've only been down here five minutes and you have just started to receive some of the benefits and none of the perks. I rub on your breast, holding each just like a Georgia Peach, so juicy and ripe, my type of woman for she wants me inside but I glide pass like a ship missing its port. I will dock but not now for these mountains of joy deserve my undivided attention, not to mention the retention of my wants to overpower yours has taken a new hold as I want to mold my d*** inside you but with great pleasure I measure my justification as notification to you that I will make you yearn for no one the way you do me, you may be far away but you will still want me, try another, they're still not me. My attention to detail when talking to you, my attention to your body when it gives me a cue, a cue to head in that direction and my erection has reached a point of full standing power to last over an hour, shower you with full hip moves to find groves in your spine like mine tilted at angles creating pleasure to your core. I do adore you and only want to satisfy you.

All from my view point ....

_____

Clear Thoughts...

Your presence calms a roving mind, your words console a confused spirit but what about me and these thoughts of insecurity that I don't want the world to see, what would they say, how would they see me?

Would they see my weakness when I appear so strong, would they see me as strong when society has a new definition but my school house verbiage is a true reflection of my direction in hopes that you detect the trueness of my words, my thoughts, my deeds as they supersede all others.

To confuse you maybe amuse you with hopes of something greater when the only thing greater is the creator and your status as I hate to say has not reached that point.

Because she could...

She was reminiscing about that one that woke up her inner beast, and feast he did to say the least but he left a wounded warrior to fend for herself with Windows to your heart down seeking a chance for closure but the exposure was too great to regulate the hormonal imbalance created. Was it that life had dealt a hand of constant deceit for defeat was not an option? How is it that sweet nothing's become something when actions don't flow as smoothly as that tongue did gliding over your nipples and the grip of a hand full of ass caused you to gasp as breath became a reaching point that seems far off? Now the circles you run trying to chase a Man not wanting to be caught but you keep running as if relationship training had provided you with a map of his mind that translated into a language only know by him. Consideration of self-starts to become into focus after determination that a lost soul not wanting to be found won't be found so the yearning of your own soul needs attention not to mention an overhauling to rebuild a heart torn to pieces as it releases pheromones for hunters as you are now considered prey but pray you must to keep your sanity for vanity and selfish right now motives can push you right back on your back as his eyes are closed and yours wide open hoping you would see what he sees and hoping it's you but the shoe being on the other foot he would probably not be in your presence so why are you present in the moment for that's all it is and the second he's done, he's done for no connection no longer exist and the kiss of fire you so much desire went up in flames when you said he lit your fire. Stand up and stand firm for your crown awaits you in the not too far off distance, just give it time and space and a whole lot of resistance. Resist your own body and the messages it's sending, a Man can make you whole, nor can he put you back together or sew up what needs mending. It's your job to figure that out, it's your job to work that out because once it's all out, and you have an empty shell call you.
T.D.

Loss for words

If actions could spell out my true emotions, would they be mixed up in various activities, not giving any priority over the other? Being at a loss for words is an unfamiliar place because words for me give life to my cells and air to my lungs. Words provide the clarity when chaos is all that exist eliminating doubt and reducing the risk of a broken or shattered heart. Some see less need for words as the need for words from one becomes a want from another but they can't be heard because of the loss of words. Some say you can be silent yet still understood, but how can you understand anything I say when you are so far gone, does it even make sense to even speak a word when it will be translated into something foul to the ear and even your presence creates comfortability issues which further increases the distance that already exist, no kiss just hugs as if a high school friend not seen in years but you know me but show me with your actions what you really mean. If a man of many words becomes a man of none what does that mean? Does that mean you took away his voice as your choice to close the door to communication or was it a revelation you pondered over and concluded that illusions are better left to the wondering mind and words are still nonexistent? Will you one day yearn for those words once spoken as sincere gestures and not a setting of posture to stand on a position of power but a true expression of one's own thoughts but you took that and threw it away as it no longer mattered but shattered that man for who he really was/is. If your tongue were removed from your mouth and you no longer had the voice to speak for your voice to be heard, would you give a second thought to giving me mine back or would pride take over and you sit back in silence and continue to show your resistance to change.

You Wonder WHY

Eyes supposedly focused on something you consider
to be more appealing all the while stealing your own
joy away as you lay there and wonder why. Your
thoughts hinder your acts of kindness but expect a
response opposite of your thoughts and you wonder
why. Your arms are folded no access granted but
you're taken for granted for limiting your own access
to love and you wonder why. You close your eyes to
the good in me but have the dearest vision when you
assume the worst of me and you wonder why. Our
bodies connect but our minds wont link as wave
lengths are blocked from negative perceptions of the
existence of something none existent and you wonder
why. Words become animated creatures thrown
about the room with knives attached reaching its
intended target with unsurmountable force and you
wonder why. Actions have motives not known by all
but intentional manipulation of the situation which
proved to permeate the air with bitterness and you
wonder why. Encouragement is discouraged as
success just may peak its ugly head from under the
cover of hard work and determination and you
wonder why. Change and progress are viewed as 360
degree turns when in all actuality it's a 180 degree
turn with my back facing you and you wonder why.
Since you wonder why let me tell you how. How to
focus on things that matter the most, let's lift our
glasses and say a toast, a toast to a

new beginning leaving the past in the dusk to live on
no more, close the door, lock it shut and throwaway
the key. Tend to my wounds with kind, genuine
words to elevate the pain and let them heal only to be
scars of the life transcended for a broken heart in due
time also heals. Be my number one fan, my biggest
supporter, my only groupie kind of sort of. Cast no
doubt and view all my actions as true for motives are
my intentions and are always meant to be true. The
change you see is progress at work a constant
improvement of the focus on goals of life which
prove to be so elusive at times but with your support
and the know that you got me when no one else
stands behind me, only on the side to see failure in
the making but you, no valley too low, no mountain
too tall, you tell me go get it, you can have it all. If all
else fails and our journey has to end, you will never
have to wonder why.

Times past and present

I remember when we would play pitch and hit off of granddaddy's barn with a cut off broom stick and a tennis ball trying to see who could hit it over the house and through the trees. I remember when video games were the past-time and not a full time activity as we would rather be outside building bikes from scrap parts that granddaddy picked up along the way. I remember cutting grass and raking leaves as a means of earning a little cash to buy candy and whatnots, and also being told to always put away a dime for every dollar made. Always enjoy the sunshine even standing in the shade. Always respect your elders and have the same for yourself. Always lend a hand for the time may come when you will need one to too. I remember the first loss in my family and the storm was just beginning, my grandfather, my mother and the devastation continued, both grandparents on the other side. My twin brother now a part of me is gone and cousins like uncles taken without notice. My grandmother and aunt gone exactly a week apart. Am I cold for thinking the way I do, has my heart become hardened by the trails of loss. I will tell you with a resounding NO, my dedication and determination to make it has not wavered not one ounce

_____

For a Man to...

The winds have to blow just right at times for you to be able to feel that man like no one else can, be able to pick his scent out of any line-up for yours is forever ingrained in his mind as if branded for life. For a Man to tell you he loves you, reservations have already been worked for you are considered a prize worth the taking and the awaking of emotion has already started for his heart is no longer guarded all the what ifs turn to why nots and that voided space in his heart has been filled with you. For a Man to grant you his heart even handing it to you on bended knee not as a sign of your dominance but the promise needed that you will care for it as your own and ownership does have its privileges and yes you are liable for any damage, just as a scrimmage match of words can be life threatening to such a fragile peace of hardware and nowhere can a replacement be found only glue to try and mend it back together but its not the same and will never be because those three words stated created a bond not an agreement to cherish it as your own and you would never break your own heart. For a Man to want to hold you and not for the moment and your movement prompts him to action and your reaction be one of bliss and his kiss make the nonexistent hairs stand up in that one place, that one space that you only want him to occupy, now you have let that man be the man as you cast all your demands in his lap and watch the stimulation of blood flow like nitric oxide swelling his veins and the only thing that still remains is a smile for you have sucked all the little life remaining and not from abstaining but remaining true to your sexual desires.

Speechless

Mumbling over words trying to find the right one to say, was it today, yesterday or the day before that I thought one thing and in reality it was something else totally different. My tongue has been tied by lies painted as the truth, yeah your truth your lie, you cry, are those tears for me or someone of your past since it didn't last you reminisce thinking of that kiss and the tears begin to roll, the thought touched your soul in ways I wish I could but your heart won't let me close enough, it remains guarded protected manipulated I mean protected did I just project onto myself my own unwarranted thoughts of being misguided in a direction you perceive to be destruction of the mind. Misguided I may be misinformed I'm not, I walk paths of broken glass on shoeless feet, the pain from the cuts are masked by the hurt in the heart especially with it being so treacherous. Speechless as I try to find the words, thoughtless are the actions that have made my moves motionless. What is gained from a passive spirit besides being provoked time and time again and no action taken, the only thing taken is my responsiveness to exchange blows as if acting as the reciprocation of force from within. Speechless as I sit deliberating my next move as my last has not benefited not even the foundation that all this was formulated on. Speechless only when I speak, my speech is taken as aggressiveness, extreme but is it, or was it, but does it, not make sense to rinse my mind with an outflow of words to clear my head or should I remain speechless and my speech sounds slurred as if in a drunken state ...

well they say a drunken mind speaks a sober heart, at least that's what holds true, but my words are stuck like glue even when given the cue to come out, they all want to depart at once and togetherness has its place and with words is not one of those times. My vocals rose high trying to reach the next note only to note that nothing was understood because you have rendered me speechless.

———————————————————

Fatherless Child

My man, you are the man. You got all that a man desires but one thing, we will discuss further as your mindset seems to drift from one skirt to another. Trying to find fault in others but take a look at yourself my brother. The face you see; do you see anything behind you? Do you hear any footsteps in the far off distance trying to catch you? Why are you running away from what's yours and trying to hold on to something that's not, let go and reach back and pick up your kids. If the choice was made for you to close your eyes today, what would people say about you? Would they talk about how great of a father you were or would they say you fathered, no you laid your seeds in many fields only to disappear when harvest time came. Now who was there to nurture their growth and cultivate their ways, guide them in the right direction and to make sure that even though raining outside they always had sunny days. You leave behind, yes I said leave behind for you have never looked back but when you do/did those same fields you sowed your seeds in will be a place of pestilence for your seeds no longer exists. You leave behind fatherless children to find their own right when they don't know their left, you leave mothers to fend for themselves but regardless their days are always brighter when they see those smiling faces but traces of you still linger, that's right, it's your bloodline that you left behind. No rhyme or reason why a beast would mate even out of season. A cycle never broken, the wheel just keeps on turning. Do you expect your boys to be men when the man they so called daddy was a nonexistent factor?

How do you expect your girls to know the difference between love and hate, because your actions prove a level of hatred towards an innocent soul, but you hope they find a soul mate, a fantasy man like you, one to manipulate minds, thrash hearts with every lash and leave fatherless children behind to find their own way but it's clear you never found yours?

For all the real fathers that handle their own, you may feel my disdain so I restrain from using my hands to forming these words not to bring light to those that run from their own but to shine light on the fatherless child's roadway as it may seem dim and chances are slim that they will make it to the other side but we see different day in day out that a fatherless child will be guided by some other hand than the one that laid down to conceive them but you do deprive them of their true bloodline. So to all of you fathers that step up to the plate every single day hitting home run after home run, I/we applaud you for it's not your effort but your duty that you take pride in daily taking care of your own.

Through The Eyes of the Soul

What are your thoughts...

Thoughtless, clueless, useless or all used up was the transmission I received from social media as it replayed comments and likes for misery loves company, and comments continue to show on my page at the same time my inbox is starting to fill up.

I have no words, no responses for negativity has already taken my mind to unspeakable places with traces of gloom but as soon as I respond, onlookers hoping and wishing for failure so they can tailor their own version of a story that has not been written.

I put the writing on the wall with no regrets, maybe some go backs, to delete what's already in cyberspace, but to no avail it's already gone and to bring it back is an impossibility at its best.

Don't put it out there, please

_____

Love You Thoughts......

All that I am is not good enough, all that I represent and I still fall short of expectations so unjustly weighed but laid in my lap as a something to pay special attention to. Given opportunities to prove my stay, quick determination that stint will be short. What are my options when I considered you to be the only one, what are my chances when I bet it all on you? I played games as a child as they challenged my mind, I still play games as a man but as enticement for excitement to hear laughs for we never grow old, to see smiles and make frowns a thing of the past. Comparison to none, from my viewpoint, I'm me, in comparison to others I still remain me. Being the afterthought I thought I would or could eventually move up the list, but my status keeps me stagnant and quiet I remain, vigilant I have become so that my eyesight can focus on you in the far off distance, but your resistance deemed as persistence on an issue I have given up on trying to figure out. I persist that you be open enough to hurt my feelings but compassionate enough to protect my heart. I ask that you take my truth and combine your reality and create a chain of communication that even though far apart they still connect. I seek to understand your ways and help improve your flaws, attract your desires to mine, and fend off any negativity. Your success I applaud; your failures I will not let you fall. I never cut you down rather help build you up, your independence well known but dominance is not a trait you display.

If I have done nothing else I have removed most doubt, I know questions still remain, they are not questions of treatment for I can treat you no better, I could take a picture and write you a letter, the story would end before it begins, the topic of the day from boys to Men. I have grown wise in my short years for sure; I have been through a lot and probably more to endure. One thing for certain I stand true to my word, I don't talk a good game I back up my word, my words mean action and I do just that, if it's something you need, you get just that. If it's something you want I give from my heart, my pockets sometimes shallow but I give from the heart. If I'm not good enough or enough at all I bow out gracefully leaving you with my words as they will always remain true as my actions are real and should provide all the evidence needed to form and win any case.

Deception

You made me feel with your words and often time your actions
followed suit. You made me think thoughts of trueness when in the
not so far distance there was none. Coincidences make doubt come
into the picture; consistency of those coincidences makes doubt a
permanent fixture in that picture. It's easy to fall prey to one sitting
in wait waiting for the right moment to steal your heart and leave
you in a state of confusion for words and actions are going in two
different directions. I can only take responsibility for my role in a
plight so masterfully put together. I gave you this but you wanted
that, what you wanted and needed all the time was not me it was the
drama and now I feel the karma of my ways which I had seen
before making me resistant to do it all over again but I did and my
outcome is the same and the future questions and answers will be
the same as such "you were the best thing ... etc.", you weren't
thinking about me so we move forward no grudges left behind as
the future is bright as the sun. My presence no longer warranted,
fights no longer justified to hold things apart all the time thinking,
we were coming closer together but the feather weight of expression
we called love was nothing more than a place holder for someone
else keeping the door forever open as no closer seemed to be in the
near distance I/you moved on to what we thought were bigger
better, the who's we thought we had but the saying two in the hand
is worth more than one in the bush.

That one in the bush hiding should have been left right there in bush for it was hidden for a reason, now you want to bring out into the light which eyes have never been able to look upon not even yours and you thought you could change that caveman mentality of brutality to a representation of you. I understand the concept of insanity brought on by confusion with the illusion of something when it's not, I call it deceit you say it's the receipt of what I deserve but on purpose you created at the same time negated all I had done to nothing of importance or it really didn't mean anything when I know deep down it did, I showed it, I kept it where it needed to be, I consistently displayed it, I sacrificed it, I gave it, but in the end you didn't want it.

———————————————————

Deeper ...

I'm deeper than the average, deeper than what you expect, deeper than what you would accept, deeper than your mind can grasp, deeper than the oceans core. So deep I clothe you in the winter with nothing on your back, deeper than the sun striking your skin with no sun tan lotion, only a notion that my words will protect you. Deeper than the last conversation you wasted your time on thinking something profound would come from a mind too small to comprehend their own emotions let alone try to take on yours. Deeper than the thoughts of you thinking that a manipulative mind can captivate the attention of many when it's only just a few (song plays "don't take it personal") I ask that you wake up to the deeper things in life, it's more than just being a man/woman, it's about finding you and understanding you when no one else will and being ok with just that and just you, if only for a little while, it's ok. Just know you are Deeper too.

<u>Words</u>

One of the greatest weapons ever used; abused, confused for something that it's not or is. It's me/you making the determination sometimes using these words to make a statement or to take a stance on what we believe. Words build up but so quickly tear down; words often highlight failures and take away crowns. Words like I love you used day in day out, words like I miss you, what's really meant at the end of the day? Were they used as deceptive tools to keep your mind wrapped around a worded feeling of security when with words your dreams become nightmares with thoughts of hopelessness? These same words can build bridges to lifelong love affairs where care becomes secondary, contrary to popular belief, there is relief in words, belief in words, faith in words, but none will do much without action.

Just want you to KNOW

The more time in your presence, I see the need for more time in the present, the present moment of making your day as you always make mine, a kiss and smile on entry and the exits no different, just we see no need to separate creating distance, not of hearts but of body's being connected. I care more now than I did before, I share more now than I did before, and I closed the door on the past and opened the window of opportunity to love and share love more than I did before. I opened the door to shed tears of joy when men aren't supposed to cry, I opened the door to compassion and truth and hide from you no lie. A deceptive spirit has walked out the door leaving honor and manhood behind and they are both closed and sealed shut, leaving me here as I am. I broke my walls down piece by piece, brick by brick only to use them to form a solid foundation, with the formation of us in mind. If you are not here, no regrets and no go backs, only looking back to see how far back you are, hoping you will catch up soon for life has not slowed down only moving faster, thought you would not let temporary temptation be your demise and cause such a disaster. With choices made and the past being where it is, no reason to speculate on the what ifs but focus on the possibilities, we find ourselves here in this moment, looking into each other's eyes not wanting to let go because you fulfill my needs without needed justification or notification, you give assurances reassuring your loyalty, you bring out the me in me resulting in miles of smiles and the occasional tear. As I shed that tear, no weakness introduced but a man displayed with vulnerabilities and insecurities so often not heard but transformed into showy renditions of fake strength when strength and truth are exemplified in that watery substance rolling down my face. As you wipe my face remember you saw me.

————————————————

BOO BOO

Why are you standing there looking confused maybe used is an accurate statement, played like the drum being beaten until the midnight hour, the tune being played is music to your ears.

BOO BOO who are you, why are you here, here to bring happiness to someone in need, is it greed, the need for speed but slow down and smell the roses as they will wither soon and lose their luster. Why BOO BOO there is none like you, none that will lay down his jacket on a mud filled hole, just so your feet don't touch the ground. Did you recognize my gesture or was it my wallet bulging out of my pocket that caught your attention? Did you look into my eyes when you meet me or were you trying to look deeper to see what senses were the weakest? The sleekness of your touch moved me in ways no one else has, that in itself was enough for me to say "she's the truth and there is no other" but eyes can't see past the other exterior for the beast lying underneath waiting to come out and devour its prey but do I stay for the feast since I'm the main dish or find a way out to save my time and energy from being used and abused by someone not so deserving.

So BOO BOO I'm not and BOO BOO I will never be, brand new you can call me but used will not be part of the equation for this calculation can't be calculated with a man like me. My calculations only conclude with positive results no negative numbers, to infinity if you can count that high.

So BOOBOO I'm not.

Need You vs Want You!

That magical line of distinguishing the difference between a want and a need. I need you in my life but sometimes I want you out, I need you by my side but sometimes I want you to step back. I need you to express your every thought but at times I want you to keep quiet and listen to the rain drops hit the ground. I need you to care for like me no other at the same time I want you to not baby me as if I'm a child, I'm a grown ass Woman/Man. I need you to be that shoulder I can lean on when times get hard, I want you to be strong enough to remove crutches and let me fall and get up on my own. I need you to be my number one fan being able to hear your voice over all the others; I want you to be able handle my success if yours hadn't come yet. I need you to be able to make endless love to me when minutes turn into hours and so on, I do want you to tell me your desires, and I need you to want me as much as I do you. I want to be your knight in shining armor; I need you to be that damsel in distress so I can carry you for a lifetime and eliminate the stress. I want a life ever after a fairytale come true, I need you by my side to make this come true. A want for more and a need completes it, as I want you more, I need you the same, neither verses the other we treat them both the same. Just understand I want you just as bad as I need you so there's no difference.

Age is just a number

Age is just a number and not a determination of maturity, just like the absurdity of the older you are the wiser you become but for some it's the opposite and an obscure figment of one's imagination that they had a revelation that they were saying and doing some grown up shit. Thinking that that pile of shit would somehow magically appear as a monument of strength when weakness was seen even by the blind and again so monumental that age becomes non instrumental in the development of a fully developed mind with the mindset of new born baby that cries a" night long and nothing is wrong only seeking attention from the aforementioned grown folks but the stokes to the ego no longer flow like the used to, now it more of a bless your heart as your sentences start with fragments of a past long gone as you try to make it part of your present but the gifts you give were taken not given as you look to the future to receive your blessing as you say to yourself bless the child that's got his/her own but how can you, when your childlike mind can't perceive wrongs of the present not to ever put the past on blast because it's not bullets that fly but your reputation taking flight to a land called nowhere for age is just a number. Words evaporate like mist and the whole point is missed not by a small margin, for marginally can be mistaken as coincidence for words mistaken but your consistency to form an opinion around something meant for failure should tell ya something, but again age is just a number.

Secret Thoughts...

Secret places, secret times, all these secrets are clouding my mind. Keeping you a secret is more than a chore, it was more of a secret need I say more. My secret I tried to keep from being revealed to world, I kept saying they not ready for someone like you. Secrets hide in dark places until the light of truth shines upon it making it the truth as well. Breaking point reached and like you being you, you came out with style, came out with grace, came out ready to conquer the world and crush it with no trace.

Where did you go?

You were lost in the moment, lost for a season, lost for what reason, lost to learn lessons, lost to make mistakes, lost to use words as my sword my defense of myself.

Where did you go?

You have been gone too long, so long I have forgotten your scent; your fragrance has dissipated to the past which I thought would last but lasted long enough to create urgency to smell you again.

Where did you go, you were right here now you appear to be on the other side of the room, the other side of the earth, your minds not right here but right there with thoughts of me lingering somewhere in the background, I wish I were in the back of your mind at least I would still be part of you instead of being distant from you in mind and body.

Where did you go, I need to share my pain? Where did you go, I need to share my gains?

Where did you go, I want to tell you where I'm going creating a path that's easy to follow, a yellow brick road leading to true happiness. But where did you go, you're no longer following my lead, for greed of control has lead you to create your own path.

———————————————

<u>My Questions, My Thoughts...</u>

Can I speak and you not take my words for granted, can I be silent and not take silence as a sign of shutting down. Can I put myself in your presence and you enjoy the moment, can I walk away momentarily and you be content with just you? Can I share my passions, my fears, and my longing desire, can I trust that you will keep these all close and closed up never to be released? Can I build a future with you and forget about the past or will I have too continually live in past, no focus on the present and the future has no place? Can I right the wrongs I have sent your way; can I correct your thinking as trust is nonexistent. Can I retract all statements that have constructed your wall, can I tear down that wall that separates our closeness and rebuild a wall around us to keep us together?

_____

Wild Thoughts...

Sometimes every now and then, every once in a while you find someone
so different, a perfect fit that you forget what it is you were thinking or
talking about. You make assumptions about them for them, you think
your right from all inclinations of appearances but are proven wrong
with the delight of feeling not lied to but truth being manifest in a voice
filled with curiosity. I think back to those occasions of deception and
you quickly remind me that you are not that one nor have you ever
been. That sleight of hand to move any piece (my heart) from its
intended place next to yours. Thinking about those distant talks with no
words spoken, wondering where you were and what you were doing to
dispose your time, all the while it was spent not in someone else's hands
but your own which kept you occupied. What is it about your
intoxicating smile and your insatiable beauty that keeps me on my toes
trying to look over walls to grasp glimpses of you? Trying to get next to
you, close to you, hold you, feel you with every sensation, my sense of
smell, touch, just to hear you breathe out air and fill the air with your
love, your joy, fill the air with you. I want to take your breath away and
you take mine, I want to feel your heart beat right next to mine.
Sometimes I wonder every now and then or every once in a while how I
did I find a jewel of sorts that shines like the sun and moon have
become one. The clear blue skies show your face in the clouds above,
the clear night sky presents stars that align your beauty; I look up and
see you all over, you are everywhere.

How can this be...

Paths created from the subconscious backlog of what ifs and why's but ties had already been bind with the mind set on one destination us, even though separated in thought we were joined already by the universe and reversal was something of the past and a rehearsal was never needed for we both knew the parts we would play, the characters we would represent, the mood, the settings all of those in place for the first showing was perfection to say the least.

Real Thoughts....

Treat her like the realest bitch you've ever wanted but couldn't have ...
How would you treat her, the realest bitch ever, clever as it may seem
and a dream maybe of all the possibilities that I could have the realest
bitch on my arm, holding my hand, command the room, VIP treatment
or mistreatment because of what's beside you, others get beside
themselves trying to get beside you to move you out of the way thinking
I'm better but you're not me and I'm not you. Lessons to learn to keep
the realest bitch by your side, if things go south for her it's no run and
hide, standing strong by my side, my ride or die, always keeping it 120
for it's a little above the norm, I agree with you, this is above all
comprehension and it blows your mind to find the realest bitch alive
and she be all mine. I treat her with utmost respect and respect all she
says and does, she expresses all her thoughts and fears to me with no
expectations, no judgment to follow. I asked her to be that person that
no one else knows or sees, that person even with faults and
imperfections, that person amused and amazed by the smallest things,
all other things so big, so superficial, so artificial, who makes these
official? Society ... society has branded you the realest bitch for all the
finer things outer, not looking at your inner. I see what they don't, I do
what they won't. I sit quietly with you just looking into your eyes, letting
them tell me what your soul is trying to communicate.

I hold you close, when they want to pull you away, my grip not tight enough where you cannot breathe, my grip tight enough to keep you from falling. I bring you breakfast in bed for you have satisfied my appetite; you bring me juice to quench my thirst after a long night of body fusion. I'm not only your man but your best friend with unconditional love and compassion, I open car doors for you, pull your chairs out so you can sit first, give you all the space you need, old fashioned my thoughts and actions may seem, how to treat the realest bitch that you have ever seen. I could give you the world and all it possesses, but all you really want is some tender affection and many heartfelt caresses. Most would perceive pleasing the realest bitch would take breaking the bank and robbing it twice, all these are given you but at what cost? And what would you sacrifice. Not to complicate matters but the realest bitch I have ever known or seen is you.

———————————————

My Assumptions Wrong

Is it wrong for me to assume wrong when it feels so right, what's left after my mind has been made up with all these assumptions, the gumption of me to make assumptions like that when they are so wrong but I think I'm right. Just tell me I'm wrong for assuming to be right, tell me I'm wrong and show me the light. This light is justification for my own short comings as I come with open arms, you show up with closed fists ready for battle when there is no need for additional blows as I have already lost this battle with tied up hands which demand me to change my assumptions, for wrong without proof is right but my assumptions were still wrong.

―――――――――――――――

Clear Thoughts...

Wanting to focus more on us has become more of a chore than the expectations of anticipation. How and when the focus left remains shut off from view as it keeps finding hiding places beneath my core, what's more is I want to find it but you won't let me with each word of deceit and defeat you make focus go ever deeper. I keep digging it out and digging out and you keep dodging me for reasons well known but being drown to you is more of a task, a mask of someone foreign, not like the day we met more like we never spoke, not words of enjoyment but annoyment to each other as we uncover deeper darker secrets not shared for being scared of the outcome but here comes avoidance of a situation that can be no longer be ignored, both our existence has been held captive from focus.

I know me

Creative in mind, body and spirit as I exude something or someone that
your past, present, and future has envisioned being the one, I know me.
I know that I could turn your world into a constant vacation, fascinated
to find out that you have not once been anywhere but in my presence, at
my place, we have not even begin to venture out pass the gates that we
have closed ourselves off to. I know I can cut and paste your thoughts,
fears, cheers, pains, gains all on one clipboard called you, to create a
masterpiece of acceptance with an abundance of care, making sure to
shape each with respect as I would expect you to openly grant me the
key to your heart. But this gesture of persuasion will only intensify the
occasion making it increasingly hard to tell you in a not so persuasive
way that I'm worthy not of a treasure that you so eagerly want to lavish
me with, I know me. Let me work to gain each part of you, let me study
you inside and out, let me *give* you all I *have* to give without reservation
but only motivation to show you what it's really like to be treated not
tricked for tricks are for the young at mind and heart, I know me. I
know my ways *have* aged and matured with the passing of time, now
being able to present to you an inquiry of sorts, but you're sort of afraid
for this view is not familiar to you so you run to safe and not so true
ground. I hear your cry as you sound off from afar louder than before,
but you were happier before you ran so why didn't you stay, I know me.

I would ask you to return but that's not my place, I would ask you to
stay, that's still not my place but I will ask you to go for my space has
grown small from an ego too large to contain, your control too immense
to comprehend, your attitude too brash to try to trim back, your *love,*
support, encouragement small and in a measurable amount, the latter
should be

overflowing but its flow has slowed and is no longer existent so therefore I ask you to go and spread your wings never to return to this tropical location they call True Man Island but set your sights on other destination spots that support or maybe distort your view for truthfulness as that's not something you see as transparent. I know me, I can, will, would have laid your heart next to mine and watch the two beat simultaneously in harmony but ...

———————————————————

Cowgirl Beauty ...

Blackness sitting high upon a throne of magnificent beauty.
Blackness sitting high for all to adore, but ignore all that surrounds you
as you bring fragrance to the air, rays of sunshine to the sky, my
goodness you're beautiful, as you sit so high.

You sit on your saddle, legs spread evenly apart, I glance at you once
more. You caused a skip in my heart. It started beating faster and
faster the closer I got, my hands wanting to explore all that sits high,
yes it includes all you want to give and my need to satisfy. Can I ride
behind you and watch your hips so fluid with every bounce, your
thighs clamp down harder not spilling out an ounce?
Your back so rigid, your spine all in line, your hair pulled back slightly,
your straps intertwine.

All these things have made more than my head turn,
my knees buckle with a chuckle of joy and laughter as I watch you ride,
no just sit right there high on your throne and let me enjoy.

Through The Eyes of the Soul

From My View Point

Baby, what can I do to put you at ease, maybe a nice long walk in
the summer breeze? Ok that's not your intention, that's not the
plan, you want to be fucked, made love to is your only command. I
can follow your direction just lead me there, I can take it from here
my hands everywhere. Gently massaging your back to release some
of that tension. Going to the small of your back paying special
attention. My palms press down and the small goes in, you say go
lower but it's your voice I can no longer comprehend, I respond to
your body as it screams out my name. I like this control thing it's
something of a game. Now fast forward to your cheeks, I smack
one with love and the other with passion, I kiss both of them twice,
she moist wanting an all-night smashin. I recognize your pain, I
refrain so focused still on your body screaming my name, it's a
game I want you to play but your anticipation of penetration is
driving you insane as you scream my name but I can't comprehend
your voice just your body as I find my way lower, as I caress the
back of your thighs, you wiggle and move about still screaming my
name. You start giving more direction but correction the path has
already been laid. You get out what you put in and soon will be
paid. You're still commanding, becoming more demanding only
putting yourself in a more compromising position as you listen to
me tell you to shut the fuck up, lay the fuck back as I make your
body talk to itself, wetness between your legs, beads of sweat on
your forehead, your eyes roll back

sending your body into a complete state of ecstasy. I am your fantasy come true, I am your tension reliever and if you're not relieved when I've completed my mission, I will kick my own a** for I did not listen. I have paid more attention to you, more than you have done in a while. I know your inner and outer most spots that make you wild. I can make you cum in minutes or just extend the time out. I touch you with fingertips of fire, climbing from your inner ankle to your inner thigh; you cry and ask why I treat you this way. Today is your day and the rest of the night too, I will satisfy all your desires and intensify those fires that burn within you. You melt in my mouth as your taste is so sweet, your cl*c so tender I can feel your heart beat. They grow faster and faster as your try to pull away but my grip so strong I want you to stay.

Photographer Unknown

_____

Through The Eyes of the Soul

Be You!

Be you, I know it's not a question or a suggestion you accept,
your actions sometimes overstated never overrated by this mass hysteria
you sometimes create but as I relate my thinking to you, I subdue all my
thoughts only to you.

Be You without some of that overweight baggage that weighs you down,
cut those straps of control and let me come in, leave the baggage outside
so I can come in. Once inside I will let you be you, scream as loud as
you like, just you be you, do what you desire, just you be you.
Hold nothing back for tomorrow may never come, its sooner for most
but for some the day no longer breaks.

Can you imagine you being you without any restrictions, no
hesitations, and no reservations? You look and appear at peace, a
release has come over you, now cum all over me.

I watch you from a distance even though close in proximity, your
conversion to you is where my interest lies, as I so gently caress your
body and those soft brown thighs. Your cries go unanswered as a
question mark never took hold, your moans a silent sigh, like ice
trying to melt on frozen snow. I want you inside out, outside in,
you be you and let me come in.

Through The Eyes of the Soul

What am I going to do with you?

Do I, want I, shall I, may I do all the things that make you smile, make you laugh, make you peek where they no longer exist, make you squirm with a tender kiss, make you think when I am all you visualize, make you walk on clouds and feel light ass headed, make you strong when you breathe my scent, my smell, your lifeline that you will no time soon release, but hold tighter as you become lighter, floating far above the clouds. A smile I see as you look down on me from a distance beyond my other eye sight, but my inner I see you up close, the most beautiful site to any human eye, do I die, cry or just melt away. What can I say, what am I going to do with you?

Keep it coming

Keep it coming don't stop, sweat flying all over the place, don't stop till we drop, drop off into a deep coma like sleep, are we sleep walking, sleep ****ing. I thought we had just completed a massive stint filled with sweat and tears good like it should be, but I wish you would wake up, you are. You just won't stop till you drop and fall off again to begin again. My energy level high I can't stop till you drop off into the darkness where your consciousness is you being laid out feeling my manhood reaching points in your body only in your subconscious, are you dreaming? No you're awake, the feeling you feel is definitely real as I steal your innocence and hide it away in the midst of my chest and the rest I let ride as it guides itself but your heart I want to control, to mold and shape and create a marvelous sculpture as it erupts with passions over flowing as volcanoes having no signs of ever cooling off. Dam don't stop, keep it going till we drop.

_____

Wild Thoughts...

Treat her like a lady when you hold her hand, caress it softly slowly even though you're a man. Rub her head gently even when nothing's wrong, always be concerned as well as strong. Communicate through words also through actions to show her you care is a greater attraction. Show me your lows as well as your highs, let me kiss your feet and caress your thighs. Point out my faults and as well as my potential, respect for each other is needed and very essential. Treat her like a lady not a prized possession, this is not love its total obsession. Lay her on the bed when dripping wet, lick the water off her body for this she will never forget. Treat her like a lady but a freak in your mind, feelings come through your fingers, let you relax let you unwind. You will want me more for I have penetrated nothing but your mind, which is enough for me as you reach that point, what point?

Internal Monologue...

Why can't I get you off my mind, why can't I get your feeling out my bones? I feel trapped, not as an animal but a creature of habit looking for that daily motivation of words which turn to actions created to be defined not be undermined by your presence, your smile, your uncanny ability to make my day or destroy my week. I am often misled by my own emotion, showing too much emotion and then it takes over until I find myself again but as I begin on this journey to be myself but that's really what others want to see, it's the other person, the other side of me which has no emotion, no need for affection, rejection is more available in these eyes and accepted because no emotional attachment connects any of the vibes that were felt before. Close the door, lock it with a key that no longer exist, one last kiss, one last smile, the door is closed but with reluctance and fear I try and I will kick it down to let you in once more. If time presented itself in any other way besides hours, minutes and seconds I would reorganize my life in a more befitting way to give you all you never had, do all you never had done, present myself as yours so we can mold around each other to grow as one. One mind, one body, one in the way of thinking, my thoughts become yours and yours become mine, no misunderstandings for our thoughts intertwine. Just a moment in time to change and rearrange time to reflect us.

I Was Just Wondering

I was just wondering how you would feel if I took you to a place your mind could only consider, where mountains are overrun with flowing rivers. I wonder if I screamed would you holla, if I jumped would you follow. Don't start this way and your first step be wrong, don't start this way if your hearts not strong. I wonder what it would take to blow your mind, to make you moan, to put a hump in your spine. I wonder what it would take to put your mind at ease, would it be the masculine touch of my hand or a heartfelt squeeze. I trust you'll make the right move and move without delay. As I have said before I complete your day. No matter where life may take you I will always be there, in your heart, in your mind, and even in your hair. My fragrance you will smell regardless who it is, the thought in your mind it must be his. There I go again back on your mind; you can't seem to release me even with the past of time. So don't try to run away, its best to run to me, because the further away you are, my eyes you still see.

Expectations

Expect no more than the body can consume,
release some of that pressure and pleasure will resume.
Expect an uprising of nature where passions are too deep to uncover,
expect me to be your day time friend and your late night lover. Expect
something less, you may receive even more, my tongue leaves no marks
so open up the door. If cracked just a little I can see my way through,
no scent or trace left behind to leave any clue. Don't open up the
door if your games not tight, it may crumble right before your eyes
by the end of the night. At the end of the night if your eyes don't
sparkle and your knees don't shake, I wouldn't have done what I
expected, just expect that not to happen.

———————————————

Clear Thoughts....

If it's anything that mattered more, it's me and you walking on a sandy sea shore, watching the waves as they hit the sand, walking back and forth hand in hand. I wonder if we sit and watch the sun rise, will we do things and be surprised. Will we make love in the sand until our hearts are content, will that make us closer because of time spent. We can lie naked without saying a word and look up in the sky for a wondering bird. I don't want you confused or ever having doubt, if something's on your mind please let it out. I'll bring you roses to maybe brighten your day, and invite you over and hopefully you'll stay. If it's anything I can do better, I'll write you a poem and maybe a letter.
7/6/94

Things Unseen

The joy of seeing today, so often not blessed for conquering
yesterday not knowing what tomorrow will bring. The sun
brings about the day; the night we still can't see. Darkness
falls only for some, but never for me. Sun shines always,
even in the midst of a storm; my shield from GOD keeps me
safe and armed. Death falls silently like a leaf hitting the
ground, the earth is my heaven where I'm safe and sound.
Death is not sorrow it's bright as the sun, for to depart this
hell and dwell with the only one. The one and only and the
thing he does, is our presence on earth, it's like we never was.

Painful Thoughts....

Don't touch my lips my lips are cold
My mouth is salty from all the bullshit told
My bellyaches not from indigestion but from your lies not
answering the question.
The question of truth, a word not known to you not only
through your deeds but the things you do. Truth to you must
have been the reason a beast would mate even out of season.
Tear out my tongue, poke out my eyes, no time for joy, just
endless cries. Cries you heard but never thought twice, even in
hot water your still like ice. My mistake quite a disaster, loves
my crime but now my master. All this anger stored inside to say
I loved to say I tried to say it's all behind me I almost lied. What
a bleep what a blonder to let me think to make me wonder.
Curiosity killed me and what I made still not happy even if you
stayed. When there's no trust soon no tomorrow, brings about
pain, brings about sorrow.

Clear thoughts ...

Clear thoughts of you based on projections of joy, kind smiles and overall being. Are you seeing what I'm seeing with eagle eyes, I hear your cries for support, not monetary nor false ties, hoping for something greater but a trueness of you wanting out so bad, so glad to find that ray of light that has shined on you from day one of your existence, you can't see it but I do and to give you a clue, look in the mirror and tell me what you see, not me but you, don't frown or look down but take a serious look at you for who you are, a star amongst stars that light up the sky. You're not dull, not shallow for the depths of your soul run deeper than any ocean, wider than the base of the earth. You are ever ending with all you have to offer to world who has never seen the likes of who, of you. Always look to the hills with your head held high, view yourself as that one and only star in the sky. Based on what I see and have gathered so far, you are who you are and what you will be is all I see and so much more.

A Description of You!

Your body is shaped like an hour glass, your beautiful smile is like a thing of the past. A priceless piece never showing age, a book never opened not knowing what's on the next page. Describing you because you're so unique, the way you walk the way you speak. Your words are like tunes from a happy humming bird, your voice so silent but still can be heard. Your step so light, your sway shows control, to see it all together is something to behold. Describing you is easily done, to make it complicated is so much fun. Your body's like brass so smooth and with a shine, knowing one day soon you will be all mine. Your eyes always shining like the hot felt sun, your curves constantly flowing like the rivers run. Your nipples are like cherries I want to eat them whole your heart is so kind now what about your soul. The thing I wonder most is not about your soul, not about your body but you as a whole.

What about yesterday ...

What about yesterday did you think about the day before when you turned your back, rolled your eyes and walked out the door. What about yesterday, was that the day when you realized, tried to size (up the situation)
Blinded by the past your eyes will never see waiting for tomorrow to set you free. I'm a man for all seasons no change just attire, more fire and too much desire.
I thought about yesterday for a moment, a quick second, closed the door shed a tear no fear for tomorrow still no thought of yesterday when I see you if I see.

My House My Home ...

My house my home my true place of comfort, somewhere to call
my own. I think of, think on this place with true humbleness of
mind, open to rejection with the projection of hope to fill that void
of not feeling like home but it is, it's mine, so I wrap my hand
around it and hold on with all my might no real end in sight, I do
see an end for it's not an illusion but a conclusion to a fight for joy,
happiness lingers near, waiting, wanting to enter but that door even
though open stays closed to this great idea of true happiness being
shattered by dreams of disruption not corruption for I will not allow
it even as I toy with it. Go away never to return for I have concluded
in my mind my house will always be my home.

It's Funny ...

It's funny how you make me smile the whole time I'm with you but frown at times I'm not. It's funny how your voice soothes my soul; my mind and spirit just the same, even lying close to you or just calling your name. It's funny how when days are long, I long to hear your voice but silence is only on the horizon, sometimes hot with disappointment but never that. I want and desire only your voice; your vocals regardless of how dismal light a fire like no other. It's funny how I miss you when I just saw you, how I search for you even when you're next to me. It's funny how I sleep and want to hold you close, it's funny how you need me more but I want you the most. It's funny how the tables sometimes turn, at first it was just lust but now it's something I yearn. I tell you all these things not as game or playing a part. I tell you these things well-spoken from the heart. Way down deep where passion only sleeps, even further down beneath where my last breathe lies, sorrow and pain and nothing but cries. It's at times like these you help make life a breeze and with you I ease into another chapter.

_____

Would you mind if. ...

Would you mind if I thought about kissing you, caressing you or just holding you like a little child does a blanket that makes them feel safe and secure or would you mind if I went down on you like an eagle stalking its prey, or play with you like my favorite toy, like a boy now a man, my hand, my strong hold grabs you with the gentleness of touch, oh you like that, as you should, I would if I were in your shoes, the news of me coming not to be next to you but lie next to you. The moans, the screams why are running, stay don't move I'm finding my grove, just to prove that you don't mind if I did all these things not falling short of completing your thoughts and reassuring mine. Confusion and passion sometimes thinking I could treat these two imposters just the same, then your name your presence bring new dimensions to the chatter that has so often filled the room but I don't mind even though danger looms. Really would you mind?

Perceptions of Mine.

Feel this way, so what happens next, a decision to be made that is even more complex.

Complex to the mind as well as the heart, how does this relationship end, hell how did it start. Let us look back to the day we met, not many words spoken, just perceptions being drawn to come to some plausible conclusion about you thinking whatever way about whoever or me.

My perceptions of you have been filled with moments of laughter, even some specs of pain. I perceive you as mine if only for an hour, your scent still lingers even after a shower. I have created for you my own secret hiding spot; the door is always open with no lock or key.

This place is yours and absolutely no one else; you have quickly made impressions that have me up all night long, thinking of your curves and all other features. You have me tossing and turning until the daybreak rises, tired and leary but energized looking forward to seeing your smiling
face.

My perception is a fascination drawn conclusion but as
time moved on you were only an illusion.

_____

Enjoy You

Legitimize, compromise, realize as I fantasize about enjoying you,

can I,

will I,

wont I

enjoy you for who you are or who you present to me,

I see you as not that or that other thing which
steps out front, only to be put back in place, no place no room remains.
You bring out the worst in me, or is it the best in me because I want to
enjoy you. If I made you the center of attention, the main attraction, I
listen for your reaction as a thief in the night, a lion hunting his prey,
can I enjoy you now and hope you stay, just a little while, your day so
filled, not with me in mind, but my mind wanting to be there too, can I
enjoy you when away, for the day, okay I get point just enjoy.

Get Out of My Head ...

Visual reflections of a silhouette seated just below my eyelid as I try to
concentrate on my own reflection for yours becomes intermingled with
mine creating thoughts just focused in the moment and each time I
blink I see and feel your movement, can't even focus as my feet hit the
pavement, almost feels like bereavement because I miss you so much,
your presence needed and wanted that much. You walk into my head as
if you own the joint, I ask what are you doing here, what's the point?
You say I brought you here and put you there, just like freewill and
choice I'll leave at your request so your head can be clear, you keep
calling me back to say sit right hear so I can put you with every thought
released always keeping you in mind. Get Out of My head for the
bedroom has no place or room for you since you have taken over all
other aspects you can't have this one too. My resistance strong but this
connection is stronger, the thought of making love to you already has
me frazzled to the point I have no more fight only a drive to bring your
body into mine to form a mind blowing bond that transcends our minds
and bodies beyond the range of man's comprehension for this
dimension surpasses even the rate of blood flow through our bodies.
You know what you can stay in my head as long as you protect it as your
own.
T.D.

Love Me Thoughts...

You remember the first day of school when you laid your clothes out, the excitement level was almost unbearable, anxiously awaiting the sun to come up. Well that's how I feel with you, so anxious to see your face, see and feel your smile, so anxious to feel your body next to mine, so anxious for our souls to intertwine.

It's a connection made for the movies with you being the star and I'm just there to support as you amaze me without even trying for you catch me out of the corner of your eye spying as you gaze into the clouds looking for that sign when it's right beside you. I catch myself at times going to an oh too familiar place of doubt, am I good enough, am I enough to satisfy your needs and my heart rate starts to speed as I anxiously prepare my mind for the worst and the first burst from your lips are words that can calm any ragging sea........you let me know you love me.

T.D.

Have you ever ...

Have you ever closed your eyes and the image you see is my reflection from the moon that peeks under your eye lid providing light to the darkness?

Have you ever had not one day go by when your presence was the only solace needed and once given it was received as a priceless gift.

Have you ever been told you were the topic of conversation in someone's head, that created a smile that creates envy for the envious, and energy for the ones that feel and see your bright vibes.

Have you ever had words said become action figures moving about the room creating a fortress for your emotional safe place.

Have you ever let your guard down without reservation to see it go up again to join up with mine as it surrounds both of us, it's called trust?

Have you ever given your heart over freely and it be accepted on bending knee as a decree that it's cherished more than life itself?

Have you ever been put on a pedestal and you keep trying to jump off as if you don't belong, when you do.

T.D.

Out of my Mind

You got me out of my mind, not trying to find mine but be all wrapped up in yours, for you have opened doors, shared your world with judgment nowhere to be found but the sound of your voice calms my soul. When so cold I was but you have got me out of my mind and I don't want to go back, not there, can I stay here, right here being able to feel your warm embrace, a release of all the things not me, for you let me be me, let me be free to create, navigate my own destiny but next to me is where I want and need you to be, let me feed you fruits from my garden of desire, drink with me from my fountain of passion. You got me out of my mind and don't want to go back, not there, can I stay here, right here. A place of tranquility not a storage facility of emotions gone bad but a release, a let-go of all the confusion giving an illusion of something that once was. Got me out of my mind trying so hard to find that person they call me, they seen him/her with a smiling face even when a fall from grace had taken hold. They saw him/her when the best of times were for some, the worst of times but a smile and a humble spirit always brought some glimmer of hope to someone seeing my smile. Out of my mind, crazy I'm not, if I ask for anything it's not a lot, just a little happiness.

Wants, Needs, Desires

Be open about your wants, needs and desires. Save the fairy tales for the movies and deal with reality when it comes to your heart. A confident woman shines like a light on a hill. But the lack thereof cannot be hidden. It starts and ends with you. It is about what you think of yourself. Self- confidence will keep you from seeking validation from a man. Remember a man will see you how you see yourself. Any man that will ever be worth your while will be attracted to your desire to want and be more. Your need for achievement will either excite or intimidate those in pursuit of you, helping you sift through the dating pool efficiently. Only an insecure man will frown upon your goals and want your life to revolve solely around him. Ambition is a force that propels you forward, and when in motion, will attract men progressing just as you are.

Keep moving.

Rejected is my middle name...

You know most of time no one knows your middle name for its something not everyone shares as if someone cares what it is. You only disclose it if requested, by that time you're vested in whatever the scenario is and the radio continues to play the same song because you put it on repeat and the emotions remain the same and if looking for change, change the station and your motivation will come back but for how long when rejection is all you've known and you paint that picture and rejection is yours as you have projected yourself there and there you remain until closed eyes become open and you see yourself in a better place, a more open space not so closed off to the world but they care even less and the stress continues to increase until eventually you're deceased and cease to exist for your name is no longer relevant, your name is now "the body".

Yes, I'm different...

Another day passes and my viewpoint still remains the same, some think it's a joke, some think it's a game but I call it being who I am not giving a dam about thoughts or opinions for they can stop progress in the middle of a step, people give their opinion but won't render help, tell you all you're doing wrong when it's obvious you're doing something right, because you see opinions are like assholes everyone has one but I can only keep mine clean, does that sound crass and a little disrespectful, sorry no apologies granted because where were you when things turned dreadful. I forgot you had your own and enough to worry about, but you still made your opinion known with your screams and shouts. Now back to the difference for I got distracted for the moment and flash back to reflect on a place I once was, any drink I took it was bond to give me a buzz and then my attitude would change, which had a direct reflection on my character as it was not built for this shit for my vocabulary became fitted with more 4 letter words and the urban dictionary was the only place they were relevant and benevolence nor grace could be traced back nowhere for I had gave people reason to form a perception thinking that contraception should have been bused before he was set free but thanks to my father above for burying the old me and transforming my mind for it had become darkness and light was just an imaginary dream. What you see now all the style and grace and no trace of yesterday because I can't look back, I can't go back because as it is I refuse to retract any statement made or deed done because they are all the reasons I am who I am right now. Thinking about making love on cabanas on the beach as we reach for the stars with the moon being the guide, come with me and let me show you, if your eyes have not seen I can show you in a dream just don't cream too hard because I want to be there too and square off within this duo called love and above all are you happy? Don't mean to be sappy but I learned my skills from my pappi.

If you don't believe who I am just leave and I'll still be who I am out of your presence and no longer existent to you. If I tell you I'll love you like tomorrow was my last day on this earth, what would say, not trying to make your day but your life and all your worries become blurry for I am who I say I am. Keep thinking different and you will be the same as others trying to play this MAN game that has your name written nowhere in it but you try to bend it to fit your comfort zone, when zoned out you are trying to become the star in someone's else's eye, not realizing that you were that shooting star that fizzled out within seconds and your life ends and depends can't hold nothing you have in. I tried to give you me, I tried to give it free but in your eyes it took two or three, in mine it took just me. Just some conversation, followed by motivation in the creation of something beautiful that you deemed dreadful which said a mouth full and I wasn't even there. You closed the door and said you wouldn't open it on my return and the statement made, burn it did, glad those true feelings came out despite being hid, so now the lid is open, am I the trash of yesterday for tomorrow's plans place no demands on me for I'm no longer wanted, no longer desired, guess my time with you has finally expired, glad you told me, glad you showed me, for love don't mean shit, not even a little bit. I thought I pierced your soul or was that the shell you presented, thought I had your heart but the windows were tinted, I would say tainted for the paint used camouflaged the hell out of what I saw as my jaw dropped to the floor for you don't love me no more, and even though sore you say, we refrain this day but every day I want you, every day I desire you and you still can't feel me, no matter how deep I get, how hard I grind, I just figured out I haven't even touched your mind, maybe he had and I'm glad you got that chance to feel love at a glance , it funny I was trying to paint you a portrait but you burned it thinking...hell I don't know what you were thinking if at all. And then again I just woke from a bad dream.

T.D.

Mind's Eye Thoughts

If words could express all my thoughts, I'd find myself tormented by a dictionary for words and thoughts translated can mystify one's mind to overturn assumptions having your words come back to you. How can one's eyesight be another's viewpoint, seeing and feeling the same thing at the same time, kind of like feeling my flow, feeling my rhyme and all to one beat and right on time. How can one's smile be so bright that any day be like sunshine when your presence is felt and the genuineness of a kiss so pure that 4th of July fireworks don't even compare for to stare into those eyes and see deeper than the surface, something else is unearthed and it's the true you as you have kept hidden your fears and tears have no place in those eyes and cries are only heard by you. If given credit for your happiness do I also receive extra points for your smile and pleasure given or even making the suggestion to keep on living for life has many valleys and mountains to climb it's a matter of choice that we chose one road over another for none are straight and maybe narrow, your resilience to conquer anything in your path just as you have my heart and a battle worth winning for my head is still spinning from assumptions made and again my words come back to me as gratitude because your attitude never changed nor did your actions, I was trying to add things up and you were working on fractions. Clueless I've been to your sincerity and the severity of the situation was I could have lost you but I found you with a package filled with an abundance of love, happiness and peace of mind and all you wanted to do was share it and have me care for it all because you give it freely.
T.D.

Scars

Knowing my past will never reflect my present and my future is not impacted but it is and has made life a living hell because I constantly go back and grab a piece of something that no longer belongs as I long for normalcy to balance out my emotions. The past has left scar tissue on my brain, not to the point of going insane but you would question my sanity as the consistency and frequency of mood swings, the lows, the highs, one moment on cloud nine the next on my knees from pain levied on myself from thoughts of unimaginable acts towards me but I'm the only one that's present to witness what's not there. Either I love too hard or not at all, my emotional attachment has an even tighter hold, for my world surrounds you as I try to stay grounded but often times you're astonished by my words and some of my deeds don't exactly match up. Concepts understood but application is my Achilles heel and once cut I become disabled to continue to love you.

Brush Stokes

Brush stokes add beauty to an already flawless specimen, brush stokes give way to all the glow that you hold so dear. Brush strokes release your pains and give gains to confidence, resilience, brilliance, all you, don't hide just provide it to the world as a masterpiece, a work of art, a start not an ending to beauty unleashed but brush strokes bring out the radiance in your eyes, the fullness of your cheeks, the voluptuousness of your lips. Brush strokes compliment your body's curves, creating angles not seen by the eye but if you close your eyes you see me for who I really am. I am brush strokes with bristles of sensuality bringing forth reality that I need that brush stroke to comfort me, console me, control me, keep me calm, arouse me, release me from all the day's frustrations. Brush strokes from your finger tips to the bend in your wrist, the attention to pay to every detail, man with that brush stroke you have so effortlessly awoken all I have in me. Your brush strokes have given power to the powerless, your brush strokes have given strength to the weak, your brush strokes have not only captured my inner being but your brush strokes have created a canvas for molding, shaping a Picasso type piece the world has been waiting to see. Your brush strokes have captivated me.

03/22/2013

Forgive me not...

Forgive me not, I confessed and got undressed leaving nothing on but my skin, you told me to pour it all out, so you could sift through the pieces, finding nuggets here and there but nothing not known for we're both grown and I have shown that I may be worth something or maybe nothing because you chose to forgive me not. Forgive me not as I unpacked my demons, letting them run free in hopes they would never return to me, for I had watched them grow into what they are beating me daily, that's just who they are. They all had names, and I thought I named them myself, they started out so childlike, not realizing their true motive was self. They worked on my self-demotivation, my self-insecurities, my self-doubt, they even tried to work on my mind to a conclusion of self-destruction, as I thought I was under some new self-construction that was tearing down instead of building me up. All this truth being told you still chose to forgive me not. My love never wavered, and my trust in you was never an issue, as I cry and tears roll down my cheek, you definitely won't console me, not even bring me some tissue, for you forgive me not and you have put me in this slot called "like the rest", but what you could not and will never consider despite being bitter I still taste good, even with all my flavor gone, I'm now as raw as they come, my heart numb to world but still beats for you, I've reduced my pride to the word it is, I've decapitated ego and rendered his head as a prize for my demise before your eyes will not happen, so I keep singing praises to Jehovah and keep on clapping for my heart rejoices as I have quieted all the background noises and you still choose to forgive me not.
T.D.

Beauty in eyes of the Beholder

Beauty not seen so often not heard
Just sway through crowds not saying a word.
The softness of your lips as your tongue glazes over, was that my
sound you heard when you looked over your shoulder?
I look into your eyes to see beauty untarnished beauty so genuine
never will it tarnish.
Your eyes reveal the depths of your soul not just outer beauty but
beauty as a whole.
Complicated beauty will be beauty not understood,
just a look into your eyes will satisfy my desires and need to
understand.

_____

Your smile

If darkness was upon me, your smile would light my pathway, that
tender kiss a que that I'm safe, your gentle touch a guide to your safe
place. Your smile makes for a long conversation with no words spoken,
a lifelong bond with no commitment given or needed as your smile and
you being who you are is all that's requested for vested interest stays in
the moment not in the future. You smile adds life to the lifeless, breath
to one seeking fresh air. Your smile is my happiness, never giving
sadness a place to stand, no demands made, just some want and desire,
once this connection was made it's an ever burning fire. NEVER STOP
SMILING!

_____

Part III

The Soul

Your eyes reveal the depths of your soul not just outer beauty but beauty as a whole.

This YOU!

This you I find myself mystified by your beauty and astonished by intellectual ability to not consider all the non-factors that don't exist but we do. You are revelation made known to few and my existence in your space is a welcome worth accepting. Inviting is your smile as it pierces through the toughest marrow, your presence resonates even with your absence as if you're still there.

I find myself trying to reason and find reasons for what is and what is not. You ask often where I came from, is it to send me back or is it for curiosity sake because where I was found no longer exist, for with the first kiss it went away. Now if you want me to go just say so and my existence will become nonexistent as your field of flowers will continue to bloom. Maybe my touch was not as deep as your caress, was it the way you ran your fingers through my hair or the way your head laid perfectly on my chest as if it had found its last resting place? So close to my heart, my heart rate slows as I place my hand on your head as if It had become one with mine, your breath, like a gentle breeze on the few hairs I have present sending them off and back again as you breathe in.

This has very little to say but so much has been said, you have opened doors awaking the dead so I keep living as advice well taken, a head never shaken as the words spoke volumes over this loud horn called life.

This YOU I ADORE AND EVEN MISS YOU MORE!

Flower of love ...

I plant this flower of love, first with a seed of gratitude, thankful that you're in my life. I water it with understanding giving space and time for this love thing to grow, even though slow at times with bumps in the road, understanding will surpass all. I sprinkle daily respect for love knows no boundaries but once overstepped the return journey can be an uphill battle, so respect love right and your wrongs will be minimized as respect is and always will be deeply rooted. I put this flower of love in the window of my heart to receive the rays of sunshine I call my love, no letting darkness ever have a chance to stop loves growth. I play melodies of your favorite to take you back to that place of peace and tranquility giving you the ability to foster your own roots. I love loving your rough edges, helping them to be smooth when I can, no changing you, nor rearranging you for I love loving you. Now the spring has come and look at you as you sit on the windowsill of my heart giving life to my every breath for the flower of love was nurtured with more sweat and tears, sunshine and rain. Now look at you as you overflow with brightness being in the likeness of a Goddess as he has bestowed his glory upon you.

_____

How strong is your love?

Is it as abundant as the fruit promised to be in paradise or is it as hard to find as trying to find clean drinking water in Flint Michigan? Is it so far-fetched that love could be right under your nose but from all the Bullshit seen and heard, you can't smell anything different? Is it that you view your friend's desperate fight for love your gauge for what love should look and feel like? What if you loved yourself unconditionally and placed no expectations on love granted and given to you because any genuine love given will be an add-on to your abundance so if it's one day taken away you are still left with an overabundance which is you.

––––––––––––––––––––––––––––––––––

Just for a moment

Just for a moment will you allow me to take control of your mind to massage out the worries of yesteryear, give you a new perspective and your mind be clear. Just for a moment, would you allow me control of your body to release tension built up to lay down a new foundation of free spirit and soul letting joy and peace reign from this day forward. Just for a moment come with me to my favorite place, your inner place and let me explore your inner walls leaving my mark on each one. Just for a moment let me caress your beauty as if it were my own, let me return all the favors of passion to release your inner beast, let me feast on your nectar like a lion devouring its prey, it won't hurt it will only satisfy a deep burning desire to be desired and admired if only for a moment.

I Love You too ...

The bearer of gifts brings laughter and smiles all the while telling one I love you and the other I'll see you later as footsteps leave tear drops to no future as the present moment seems so right even though wrong with all my transgressions left at the door when I walk into a cloud filled room not being able to see my own hand in front of my face let alone see clarity for I'm as blind as the next man trying to find his way back home but if I don't walk out now I never will. I love you too were words spoken daily as the good mornings and the good nights before I closed my eyes only to open them to screams of my own conscious trying once again to bring light to an already dark and damaged soul. I love you too more than words could ever express, so I dress myself in the clothes from yesterday hoping today no one would tell the difference because I changed my shirt but I never changed my mind so the change I so eagerly sought after was once again an afterthought because confusion was my only friend and based on all the statistics it would be my end if I didn't love me too.

_____

If walls could talk

If walls could talk would they tell stories of betrayal when loyalty was the expectation. If walls could talk, would they speak a language of the unknown but known by most but they only speak it behind closed doors. If moans and screams were understood by another to be silence and separation, what would the walls have to say about the lies told to give reassurance when all the time the walls knew the truth? If the walls could talk would they show the marks of handprints, scratch marks from an evening of passion not knowing pain would soon follow trying to fill a void that will always remain hollow. Hollow from an emptiness that can't be filled with shallow words of deception to give the perception of what's not when reality was already known and understood and character would have never been assassinated better yet demonstrated a stronger you but the walls do talk even when silence seems to be the only thing heard. If walls could talk, would another language be spoken to hide the real language being spoken? If walls could speak would a new year bring change when years before it was just a resolution and no solution ever reached. If walls could talk would they reveal your true intent when you thought, you were the only one who knew and no one else especially that one had a clue.

Thank you

Thank you for this visual of change, thank you for this time to rearrange my thoughts and get back to me. Thank you for the acceptance, allowance and appreciation of me. Thank you in advance for the past, the moment and a future yet undetermined is as bright as my imagination will uncover.

Thank you for the lesson of intolerance when tolerance would have been a better option, thank you for a second chance when there were no more remaining and the thought of entertaining a fragile mind and setting boundaries never to be crossed again. So I begin with a thank you from the bottom of my wide open heart and soul for as long you stood there I would still be here but you moved and forced me to move but in a different direction with different projections as reflections of change for the better not for you but me. Thank you for closing the door and locking me out, for changing the codes and shutting me out. Thank you for letting me get me back as your intention was never to have me at all. Thank you for the reality that I no longer need you but want you even more, for setting me free so we both can soar. Soar to new heights for if we stayed we could never move, and if we moved we could not stay so we move and here we are in the moment, so let's stay here in mind but keep our feet moving so not to miss a special moment in time as it waits for neither one of us.

Thank you for a new understanding of self because a grown man should already know so lost now I'm found with a new perspective on being in the moment, staying in the present for the past nor the future have no barring and caring becomes less but means more. Thank you for detaching, as I would have remained attached and not in a positive way, so thank you for the way made as the light at the end of the tunnel is well in view. I visualize you, I appreciate you, I accept you, I claim you not as my own but a piece to be held briefly, so I thank you and most importantly, I live you ...

Through The Eyes of the Soul

It's morning ...

The sunlight dawns a new day and I'm still here. The sun goes down and I'm still here as reality sets in only to realize my body has laid next to a lifeless soul and my goal to achieve magic has turned into a nightmare of twist and turns, games and shows of Power when the last episode has since been recorded and discarded as playback too many times it can't. It's morning as I wake to drama filled moments of accusations from one's that only know my name, know my face but have no idea who I am and what I represent but their word is bond and the bond you have created will never be broken as the day will soon come when conversations will turn to words of distrust a mad day of sorts trying to sort through the reasons for treason, but that season has now passed and the bed you made, made comfortable when the unthinkable lurks in the shadows to open your eyes to what was, you asked me why and you should have posed the question to the one posing the question but your answer has eluded you like the plague, you seek no refuge only further confusion. You lay down ultimatums as stones never to me moved, but they too are not permanent. Just as it's written in stone it also fades and washes away unless preserved with care and understanding of the elements, let it stay outside too long and it creates its own developments from the elements. Cast a stone of fury and not expect a returned blow just as vicious is delusional, transcending even the most complex of minds. Its morning and when you wake I hope to be a figment of your imagination.

<u>Honest Thoughts...</u>

Temporary lapses in judgement result in a lifelong scar to be remembered just like it was yesterday. Pain like crushed velvet never to be smooth again, no pressing out just pressing forward leaving behind a love found but now lost again not in my hands but by my hands and I can no longer hold on for my grip is no longer strong enough. All my energy expended on never found expensive perceptions I called deceptions or were they, that's the perception it gave as I became enslaved to finding them true and the whole time missing the whole you. I would often go back in time and find that place where trust and respect resided only to find they had moved on too leaving me without a clue and I still tried to stick around like glue but you knew how close the End was because the shoes you most times wanted me to wear, I knew they were too small and I still had the gall to want you to put on mine and in my mind they fit you perfectly. Pulled all the tricks out the bag which lagged consideration for maturation had not taken place and now a race to the finish to keep you from crossing because once you do I will completely lose you and I don't want that.

UniqUE ...

A man of many talents, flaws, and anything else you want to add to the mix, but help me to fix my flaws and improve my talents before packaging and discarding me as a thing of the past. Sometimes we discard things of value because they appear to have lost their luster and shine; we sometimes think that the more something shines the more expensive it is. All the time not realized that what you have/had only had a little dust on it and needed to be dusted off, polished a little bit but you know what you have. It's that uniqueness that keeps me who I am, it's me being me that keeps me unique. I may not stand out in crowds, but when my song plays there is a split like the red sea. I give all I have and expect nothing in return and that makes me unique, I pay attention to your wants and needs even as we speak. I listen to your words, your tone and with no conclusions drawn I uniquely act. Uniquely acting, so easily detracts from my uniqueness to be made common even when consistency shines so bright its blinding. Consistency of actions, no directions needed but it's about what you need, what you want your humble voice roars, I listen. I think of you at times with no thoughts of myself, losing myself in a moment and coming back to see I'm still standing there with a bewildered look on my face. No trace of me just blank stares into space; eyes wide shut not seeing the truth even with it being right there in front of these glazed over eyes. Tears fall and clarity starts to appear from the distance, but with pain being the first cloud to be held over my head, but walk a little further more clarity appears and the sun starts to shine, realizing my uniqueness once again, that I am like no other and I am no other, not even my twin brother and I are just the same. I'm the one looked over but once passed over there is no looking back, the should haves, would haves are all what could have been, now you realize how unique I am.

Black Tie Affair

Introductions made with no spoken words, eyes looked through to see the depths of the others soul. Conversations had with our eyes being the main source of reaching out. Black Tie Affairs when everyone put on their best behavior but you misbehaved badly but I gladly accepted and returned all you bring to view. Your attire something to admire with thoughts being kept only to me for disclosure could be closure to openness felt just for my eyes only. I saw your walk and sways of perfection as if gliding on air and your intoxicating scent had me following you with my eyes all night even when you departed I started to think of you, your whereabouts and talked about you in my mind from that day forward. Now fast forward to this day, I still look into your eyes with the same intrigue and admiration, gender gaps separate us only to give us a flawless connection of mind and body. Thanks for attending the Black Tie Affair.

Love Your Beauty

Affection so easily given with no reservations no hold backs, affection overflows like rivers being taken over by the open seas. Grant me that piece of your heart to provide a place of protection, grant me that piece of your heart that guards us both from rejection. Regard draws me in closer and care holds me tighter, your smile illuminates a path to your heart, and permeates your beauty from within. Conviction stands behind you, keeping guard of your integrity making trueness of word and action a foundation for your being. Adoration of your blemishes making your curves flawless and the gentlest touch can smooth out all the rough spots. Picture perfect or paint a perfect picture of beauty inside and out, a picture being painted with the eyes alone can seem amazingly complicated but you being underrated for it is stated that beauty covers over a multitude of imperfections.

Through The Eyes of the Soul

The Taste of Cognac

Poured over a glass of ice to let it sit and marinate to the state of consumption making no assumptions about the taste, for its pure like you. Just as cognac sits in barrels for years being aged to perfection so are you just as deserving to be celebrated when your presence is known to man. The taste is one not all can bare, just as your grace, your love, and your care. Your intoxicating ways are taken one sip at a time, savoring ever drop to the point even the ice flows with your every swirl. Just as cognac you should never be taken for granted, I should never get tired of taking my time with you, consuming your words and getting high from your love. Just like cognac, you calm my mind and warm my soul, wanting so much of you I lose control. The bottle has a bottom but your heart knows no end, so I promise not to waste one drop of it as you pour out all I hold scared and will always defend. You are woman and your every fiber should be treated with more care than a thousand-year-old barrel of cognac to be treasured and put on a shelf where all eyes can see. Your beauty should be admired and cherished beyond your wildest comprehensive, just like watching the finest cognac being poured over ice. Lastly I say cheers to you for your strength, your character, your beauty as we celebrate you today and every day.

Signature Drink of the #urbancowboy
750 mL bottle Hennessy V.S
1 cup Grand Marnier
1 cup Fresh Squeezed Lemon Juice
1 cup Simple Syrup
8 oz Sprite
2 quarts Iced Tea
3 oz Peach Schnapps
Garnish: Lemon, and Orange Peels with Peach Slices

Method: Add all ingredients to a large punch bowl with 1 large ice block, allow to chill and serve.

Flowing Thoughts...

As I strive to be all I can with an attitude that fate has no hold on my future, I am reminded daily that my fate is determined by my actions or non-actions creating reactions of regret but regret gave choices and the remorse's fall on deaf ears for you heard the sound of failure, whether it was failure of heart or failure to succeed, fate had already planted a seed whether watered or not, it was still gonna grow, gonna show up and show out. My presumptuous attitude at times has caused confusion, my own to be exact, my miscalculation of a near future was further in the distance than the eye could see, a mirage of happiness had placed a tree of life within eyesight but the reality is/was it was nothing there but space only filled with the hot air being heated by the sun above. I continue further on this journey called life to find that the most precious things are not things at all but people that hold you up to sky as a sacrifice to the father for you are a prized possession to them, willing to give you up, willing to lose the most important part of them. No hidden agenda just love, no malice of heart just love, no preconceived notions just love, with all these imperfections and faults being displayed in front of you and yet love conquers all. It has conquered a beaten but not broken heart, a grimy fleshly body covered in the world's demise but through all that you still loved me. I use this pen to show and give credit to you for at times it may not flow off my tongue like a cascading water fall, gently reaching the crest of the bottom but creating mass confusion near the bottom and a calmness on top, with grace the two meet to settle differences.

For the moment

Can I reach the corners of your mind and stay there and take up that space no one else can occupy and supply you with endless thoughts of us as I thrust my all into you leaving none of me behind. As I talk and think about this love thing, my heart starts to sing and rejoice as I have no remorse for loving you the way I do for the person called you has me doing things I wouldn't normally do, well I lied as it seemed I tried to minimize the size of my love for you. Its moments like this that I want to get all in your head and create a mass hysteria of happiness, laughter and joy and pour it all on you until you can take no more and even then my love won't stop flowing as I want to keep showing and enjoying the simple things in life with you. Waking up to sunrises as they provide no surprises just the beauty that God has made. Holding hands walking the shores of beaches unknown to stop and let the waves massage our lower as we caress the stress away from the upper and low and behold we are one as the sand is removed and we sink deeper and our hearts rise with the sun.

Tomorrow's Thoughts...

Time elapses time as your days become shorter and your presence cease to exist. Time even though posted on the wall still runs out, time even though we watch it all day long, it still runs out and so is life we watch ourselves sometimes being in situations and when we decide to change time has run out. We so often hear, he/she has changed their ways but time ran out. We make time for those and things most important to us, but trust time will run its course and run out before the night's end. Daily smiles, showing love to the ones you love is time well spent, for a frown is a waste of time, that moment lost never to be seen again, was it really worth my/your time to be given to such ill weighted feelings. A lifetime could be seconds to those who only briefly opened their eyes to a brand new world but time ran out. A lifetime to the average is taken for granted that I/you will be here that long, not realizing our time has been running out since our birth into this world. Why not make the best of this short lifetime, impacting others the way they impact us, giving to others and not expecting anything in return but a smile of gratitude. Tomorrows promises can and will disappear as quickly as the last memory you thought about. Make yesterday's failures today's successes, for tomorrow may cease to exist with the passing of time. Life's too short to think about the should haves and would haves, think and live in the moment, giving thanks every day for another day standing, regardless of the struggle you are still standing. Smiles bring joy even in the midst of a storm, blessings are shelter from above, and your shielded faith is able to win any battle without throwing a punch. Happiness granted, respect always earned, passion for life observed, a peaceful spirit seen as a shining beacon lighting the way for many, so use your time wisely.

Sincere Thoughts....

I tell you my deepest and my darkest hoping that you would conceal my pain but you feel the need to reveal my pain and bring to light all that is darkness. So why the silence, when you ask where did my sharing disappear to, no it's still there but the glare from all the exposure you have exposed me to has created clouds of doubt and thunderstorms of misguided communication. Criticism towers over the conviction I have to move in any direction besides the one you have set forth, but how can you guide a man that needs no guidance, your opinion is often valued and given more credit than received but deception is felt when actions are contrary to your view point. My life story is not filled with arrows that turn around like boomerangs to come back and haunt me again, or to be shot off again from the mouth that was a listening and understanding ear that I held so dear. My life is not a weapon formed against me, but one that has taught me the value of us.

_____

Black Man to Black Woman

Daily pains from the past ring out like yesterday busting our ear drums over and over again. Daily portrayals of black men as beasts walking on all fours with the world looking at us like we're some mystical creature that one day suddenly decided to walk upright with no direction in mind, a lost soul if you will but even if we prove wrong all around us, we are still looked at as beasts walking the city streets ready to devour and destroy anything in our path but that's the worlds mindset and we still try to prove them wrong day in day out, and only hear that our outcries become muffled to be seen on social media as social injustice and still no justice, it's just us, us against the world.

And you wonder why our days seem so long, and frustration is taken home with us not to lash out but to be laid down at the door step, coming through a door of peace and understanding, demands increase and words degrade to beat us down even further creating more distance as resistance starts to churn in a soul that seems to be all alone. We just need, we just want; we just do what we can. If you are my right and I your left why can't we walk in solidarity staying in step the whole way, if you see me step up don't step back because my failure along with success depend not on you but with you we can accomplish more than the mind can comprehend. Is there some mystery behind what we see right now, no the mystery was revealed years ago by Willie Lynch, and even after reading we are still abiding by the same rules but without the same restraints, now it's our minds holding us back? Often times we are beaten with a professional whip, hoping to come to a place of comfort and ease of pain but the total opposite being words like salt added to wounds still fresh from the days thrashing.

Please ease my pain don't intensify my pain since rain has masked all my tears, pride has silenced my screams, sleepless nights have controlled my dreams. All we wanted you to do was listen to us, talk to us, encourage us, lift us up not hold us up, respect us for the world has none, build us up when the world tears us down, place our crown's on our heads when we walk through the door and all these things will be given back to you multiplied by twenty and plenty more.

Black Man to Black Woman, Real Talk Let's Talk.

How is My love?

My love does not compare nor compete with even the best of them, I win every time as My Love is stronger than heavy chains wrapped twice around the nimblest pole, protecting it from all elements seen and unseen. My Love runs deeper than the oceans core with the sky being the ceiling transcending far above the clouds. My Love is often taken as a weakness for the blind heart sees no danger just the grander in all it touches and extends even when there is no one reaching back to hold on to it. My Love extends far beyond the grave as I become enslaved to my own feelings of distrust but My Love says entrust in those you hold dearest to receive and believe in the something called My Love which is complete with days of joy and laughter and nights filled with passion and romance. Take a stance on My Love, it provides strength even to weakest heart. Take a glance at My Love and I will watch your eyes glaze over not from staring but mesmerized as trueness has become a thing of the past. Take a chance on my love and your winnings are automatically doubled from no investment at all. But if My Love appears to be too great it's never too late to walk on by (song plays), and I will play a song for you as you would have missed the opportunity to share My Love.

(Our Love ... instrumental plays) ... (Walk on By ..Isaac Hayes)

Your Actions

Reacting to resistance and a means of control, transformed my actions not as excuses for abuses of your mind nor your body but my actions were true reactions to what I didn't want or so I thought. Your actions have taken you down roads less traveled and now you see why, taken you over mountains when flat land with a shorter path was right there. Your actions created glares which turn into stares from ones that were once admirers now adversaries on the side of one you acted out against. Your actions have multiplied as if breathing life into a man with no upbringing, no guidance on how to be one, be the man. Your actions are true examples of the one life you live, if you chose to give it nothing, nothing with be your return, if your actions prove you worthy of the world all will be given to you in due season but really what are the reasons for your actions.

Wondering Thoughts...

Are you the kind of woman that can take my words and make them your own, take my expressions to form an opinion, take my actions not just as gestures but the formation of a foundation built to last? Are you the type woman that tries to tear your man down to build him up only to find what you transformed is one misinformed and misguided or maybe one that sidesteps your advances to move on to someone else. Are you the kind of woman that demands perfection even when your direction is flawed? Are you the kind of woman that holds onto the past only to delay your future? Are you the kind of woman that keeps count of how much I don't, instead of seeing and witnessing how much I do? Are you the kind of woman that caters to your man as if he were a king, hell you're the queen you both sit on the throne together side by side, hand in hand but for some the demand to be so independent limits your dependence on a man that wants to give you world, but the clauses in the pre-nup limits you even more with your independence growing to a state of loneliness thinking you have no one else to depend on but yourself but he's still there waiting, but for how long? You should be the kind of woman that stands beside her man but be willing to step back behind your man to hold him up or at least cushion the fall. For failure falls on both, so if we fall together, we get up together, we become stronger together, there's no separation, we have been through too much to let go, we can now look pass the trees and see the forest on the other side. Are you that kind of woman?

My Best friend

My best friend, my do or die kind of chic, my forever loyal, forever forgiving, never changing character, just growth over the years, many tears shed but most of happiness for some things seem unreal and unattainable but we see every day as our conversations never stop by request only for rest to catch another breath and start again. Your words keep me motivated, your responses keep me captivated, your body language speaks volumes and silences even the loudest crowd. Conversationalist yes, no words go unsaid regardless of the subject; we subject ourselves to open judgment hoping that understanding is the end result. Limitless yes are the boundaries that surround us, we create our own hurdles, some taller than others but we always get over, I first climb to the top to pull you up and you go down first as I guide your every step to safety. My best friend even if our paths are separated we cross paths again and again getting updates of old and new and part ways with smiles as the first day meet. Grant me one wish from which all your dreams come true, grant me two and beyond the clouds is your destination, my imagination your canvass to do as you please. I grant you access to my deepest and darkest secrets all the time knowing that my future is so much determined by my past. Not all outcomes are bad and not incomers into your life are good but funny how life has a way of teaching lessons if we only listen, a way of showing us the road less traveled if we look beyond ourselves and want the best never the worst for the other side for our side can only become stronger for two will always be mightier than one. I speed by my own faults to see yours as greater than mine but in reality, my faults are too large to get to yours so I paint pictures with my own perceptions and deceiving even the most solid of thoughts to cause contemptuousness when there is no need, creating separation when we are so close. At the end of the day my best friend overlooks with open eyes my ways as a way of getting out of my own way.

Selfless

Outward magnificence being nurtured by inward purity of self only preserving stages of life for growth. Your smile adds the pleasantries of body oils leaving your fragrance to be consumed for years to come. Your caring nature gives natural medication to the sick at heart and mind; and brings life to that which was once given away to sorrow and demise. Your passion to understand replaces the need to be understood, for your grace explains it all. The innocence of your mind leaves no room for manipulation only truth of thoughts. You give the weakest link strength to carryon to a more encouraging tomorrow. Your clever use of words, quick-witted responses only add to an already beautiful personality. Your love so intuitive paying attention when attention would normally not be in the present but present you remain, the same you remain, and the love you share is almost insane. I love you being you.

————————————————

Consumption of Time

24 hours in a day, 8 to 10 spent working, 8 hours for taking care of business and adding some leisure on top, 8 hours to sleep is the preferred plan but all these hours not a minute passes that I'm not consumed by thoughts of you, my mind wrapped all around you, it gets even more confusing as I try to conceive or retrieve other thoughts outside of you. I have consumed my mind with time left concentrating still on you, where are you, how can I find you, what can I do for you, you are my consumption of time. Now time does have limits, it runs out daily and with thoughts of the day ending sending me into a frenzy for all the things I did not do with my time besides concentrate on you, but you on the other hand, wisely used your time to find time to say hello when time permitted, remained committed to all commitments no change of reservation, still on schedule but time for me has run out and starts again the next day with you on my mind.

A Walk on the beach

Walking on the beach hand in hand, catching each other's smile as we turn back and forth, eyes trying to stay focused forward but keep coming back to that smile. But for a while I felt like I was in a place where no one else existed but us, no one else mattered but us. Picking up sea shells, looking at their beauty as sand had worn them down but worn they were not, fragile maybe but still strong enough to hide life and protect it from the elements. I see us in the distance, walking hand in hand, side by side, almost sounds like we are at the alter about to kneel and profess confess our love for one another, for there is no other that makes me feel the way you do, makes me act the way I do, just simply do the things I do. I glanced out the window only to see the moon being comforted by clouds; they so gently made the night air feel warmer even with a brisk breeze coming in off the ocean. I lay down beside you to grant you the same option as the moon, let me be the clouds to cover you all over, caress every inch of your body, and hold you while sweet rest falls upon your wary head. Just take a walk with me and see where it leads.

Brighter Days

Tears of pain bringing out sunshine after the rain, but the pain still remains, not remnants, but as a deeply rooted tree not wanting to give up ground for it has laid claim to what it considers to be rightfully his. To the dismay of others as I watch from outside myself a transformation taking place, my mind and body react differently but in sequence to the events that have taken place. My mind trying to figure things out, my body trying to run from the situation, standing still is my position with no transition to a better place only remaining in this place, I got to do something and do something quick, I'm losing myself, if not myself my mind because it's all intertwined in confusion with an illusion that all will be ok but it's not. I got to move, I got to do something and go somewhere from all this madness that has found me, now surrounds me. I dream of brighter days, I visualize the sun shining down on my face as days of old, I see the old me coming back with a twist, being remiss to repeat a saga that has consumed me from the start, my heart not wanting to let go but I caress my own, and realize on my own that this is not where I want to be, I change, have changed but remain unchanged from who I was, who I am. Today is a brighter day.

Emotional Thoughts...

My desire has reached a point of uncertainty with little focus on possibility. I look around and realize I don't have me to continue a legacy, one that looks and acts just like me. Is this one of those times in life where something small could be and make such a difference in your life? One that could slow my out of control lifestyle or at least calm me to a point of being in control. I could see it now, me and he/she, it really doesn't matter for life alone is not one that's sought after nor is it granted much support from my peers but my fears hold the most control making my mind see outcomes that in a dream will wake you in a cold sweat. The thought of being deceived into thinking you are as great as they say you are, are you?

Are you the soul provider, the life giver... no you are just one of the many that have posed the same question time and time again? If granted the opportunity would I cease to exist for my desire has taken on a look of their own, he/she looks like me and somewhat acts like me but is this me.

Infinity

Continue this journey with me through clouds of confusion, no illusion but intrusion by others to see and find what we have. Infinity is the time I have set to keep you close to me or until you decide to stop the clock but mine has been repaired and indestructible throwing away the key never to stop ticking, like my heart beats with life, your breath, your presence gives life to my smiles, gives reason for my season, provides sunshine where only darkness lies, provides joy and replaces the cries, provides a hiding place where danger lurks. Things will never change but change is inevitable, so with that change I will bring range, range of motion and emotion to follow you wherever you are, if not physically I am always present when needed and greetings will give the reaction that gains traction to last that much longer, the closer I come to you, the stronger I become for you. Our coexistence on the premise that we are who we are with no misconceptions about the other, whether lover or friend we will not pretend as we exist together to infinity and being granted eternity we are fraternal twins attached at the hip when you fall I slip but never losing hold of you ... I got you and will never let go even if you go in another direction, be guided with the type love that we have shown each other whether friend or lover. Far reaching to ever touch the stars above but we can lift each other to heights unknown, to depths never discovered. From those depths is where I discovered your endless flow of love so freely flowing only knowing my hearts desires, creating burning flames and raging fires. Don't let it end.

Rendezvous

Slipped off to a place where eyes no longer have vision of what is and there are visions of what could be. A rendezvous is taking place, taking you places that from your minds viewpoint it has to be a dream. We agreed on the time and the place, the place was still off in the distance becoming closer as miles become yards and feet become inches. Here we are, me and you alone together, what do we do with ourselves, you have made yourself available to me and I to you. Do you treat this moment like any other or even bother the thought of it having to end, no we just pretend, there's no end? We just connect, and the energy that reflects off of two shining stars has an effect on the naked eye, causing noteworthy pain that needs to be documented for things like this don't happen all the time. The moment you speak, I process your words as food for thought, nourishing my soul's innermost hunger, you have satisfied my thirst and what's worse is I'm no longer hungry but starving for all of you. I have the appetite of the King I am, wanting to feed off my Queen, your skin my plate, your wet spots my filler, your soft spots my desert, a five course meal you are with all so wondrously prepared with the hands of the Father. I sit back and admire as my manhood transcends higher and harder like day and night fighting for space, that hard line drawn in the middle is me standing with lightning bolt in hand waiting to cause a thunderstorm of sorts within your being, turmoil based desire, a cry for me as you scream my name, your legs can't stay closed as the fire is too intense for them to find each other again at least not now but the coolness of my tongue brings relief, then a release of volcanoes erupting, then .... you know what we still have not reached our rendezvous point, no time no place intended but our minds have been there and back.

Missing You

Missing you today is like missing you for a lifetime, waiting for your call, waiting to hear your voice, waiting to be in your presence, missing you like crazy. Am I crazy for missing you like I do, am I crazy for wanting to be next to you, beside you, holding you close, and you wonder why I don't want to let you go. The distance brings me closer; the miles are turned into feet but the far between is still there yet I still feel close to you. I hear your voice as soothing to the soul, I hear your whispers as my inner desire takes hold ... come close to me, come close to me is all I can think of with distance not being an issue but just waiting on your arrival, a true sign of survival just waiting. I love you close and yet love you just as much when land, air and water separate us to the upmost degree. I see your presence, I feel your presence ever so close, come back soon 'cuz I love you.

———————————————

Soul Food

Food for thought to fill you up, mashed potatoes, collard greens and
other dishes, and a jar of sweet tea now take a gulp.
Food for thought refreshes your soul, a mountain of love
and tenderness and now you feel whole.
A little bit short of being totally complete, will I fill that same void
when we meet?
Or will that void grow larger, and you step back faster,
will you look at me and say what a disaster.
We both know the conclusion and to stop the confusion it won't be
an illusion when you call me your master. I won't take your soul for
you deserve so much more, more than a long night of passion where
all rules are broken.
Just blood, sweat, and tears and continuous stroking. Your finger
nails in my back creating trenches of satisfaction, my reaction goes
deeper with every stoke scream, moan, a king on his throne as you
have been conquered, but no worries my love I hold your heart as
it's mine connecting the two in mind to listen to our heart beat.
Once again I've spoken, once again out of turn the louder I speak
the deeper you yearn, you yearn and long for something you've
never experienced, an experience that you may long for even in
your sleep.
Don't toss and turn and don't call out my name, once again please
remain discrete, for a silent mouth and an open heart receives all
desired, but a running river soon overflows washing away banks
and structure is lost.

mon amour pour toi (my love for you)

It feels so good, feels so right, holding you caressing you all through the night. Looking into your eyes to see deeper than you feel, looking a little further to know those feelings are real. Creating moments so intense, levels of happiness reached and exceeded, transcended above the clouds, cloud nine you have soared over with ease because pleasing you is so easy, and so second nature to the touch, it just feels so good, it feels so right, holding you close, holding you tight. With the passing of time, all moments so precious, being precise with movements, trying to leave an impression that will be an expression of how I really feel a feeling of something real but surreal to the imagination but real to the touch and I love so much the continued progress of long term smiles, life long memories that have created a longing to hold you close and hold you tight early in the mornings and all through the night. You make my days want to be filled with your presence; your existence in mind is always dominant, dominating my thoughts as I think of you constantly. My focus on areas outside of you always lead back to you and the pathway seems clearer as you become closer but closeness has its place and placed on my heart a stamp with your name all over it. At the end of the day as the moon begins its assent to the sky, I see your face traced in the shadows, I see your hand reaching out to me, I hold out mine to grasp a hold of all the love you have to give, can I hold you close, can I hold you tight, if not all night at least a little while.

You got Me

You got me once, twice now this third time a charm, this third one is going to hurt and bring about change. You got me thinking one way when all the time it was another, you had me pinged for a friend not your weekend lover. You got me confused about my feelings and which direction is up, at that perplexing place do I go or do I stay, no love remains at the end of the day, it was poured years earlier and never replenished, it all went away and now it's diminished. It's not for no one else I do it for myself, confused and at a loss for words to say to make things better but communication non-existent, all words taken for granted and completely scrutinized never rationalized in a mind that wants things one way.

Waiting for You ...

I stood quietly in the corner no one noticed me but you, I smiled you smiled but I waited for you. You handled what you called your business but I waited. You greeted, treated all your onlookers with such grace but I waited. I caught your eye being caught by another's eyes besides mine, I still waited. Having thoughts of betrayal and thoughtlessness but blessed be the child that got his own, my own mind to make decisions at the spur of the moment, creating movements in my bones to move from that spot of waiting, no longer hesitating or meditating on the next move for my groove had taken hold and as bold as I wanna be, I walked up to you and said. "Tired of waiting, no longer hesitating on making a move for I feel the groove of your body and mine making sweet sounds of lustful joy, bring a toy I'm a boy I'd like to play with you as we go deeper to find out what really makes you move. Is it my hips rounding corners (your hips) or is it the way I throw your legs around my neck and you subject yourself to a night, a moment (long time) of complete pleasure, your measurements will never equal up, nor compare so don't dare to compare me to no other for I am the brother that will rock your world, make you want to tell your girls, he's the one but you can't because I'm still waiting quietly, silently for you to make your mind up on what you really want.

My Sentiment Thoughts...

I don't mean to be blunt or maybe I do, it's something I have grown to like over the years, it helps keep down confusion giving no life to an alternate illusion of what ain't. I ask for the same blunt force of words forcing me to face simple truths about myself that at times may be truth and other assumptions made on the part of the other half in some cases a quarter, no you're no part of me for you've given not to me, no I don't think about the other, not a contender just a reminder of who I am, what I'm about, where I come from, what I was taught, what I retained and applied, what I've accomplished, what I've tried. No comparison needed, none even drawn, impeccable qualities ignored, signs of greatness looked over like the passing of time, none of these matter for your heart in its traitorous vain makes a decision to take my breath away in awe, really is that what you chose, sounds like you're giving up to lose. Out of character, way below your stature, you've grown but in what direction. I thought you had set a course of happiness but it seems your mile marker has not been planted to let you know you have reached your destination so you continue for what, for who, for not it seems, your dreams become nightmares, your days filled with cloudy skies, gloomy nights no star filled skies no way to wish upon a star, they are not there but I am right here. I was in front of you, now I stand at a distance, not waiting for you to come but waiting to watch you pass. I will encourage you as your journey takes you places not in a dream, keep your head high, move forward, I scream "I believe in you" believe me that was hard enough to come off my lips but who I am, what I'm about, where I came from, what I was taught, what I retained and applied gave me the courage to be able to say it from the heart with no ill malice intended, my heart has mended, but feelings of rejection give way to reflection to move forward from this place, still can't erase your existence in my mind but in time, yes time heals all wounds.

Caramel Coffee

I drank a cup of you, only to realize I could not only drink just one. I drank another cup only to realize I couldn't only drink two. The first cup so refreshing with a twist at the end, you can only take it away, after that it depends. Was someone else having sips or was I the only taker, I'm confident in myself how else can I shake her. The second cup was better, even better than the first, no need for clear spring water, its caramel coffee to quench my thirst. The more I drink the more I need, going back once again, am I showing signs of selfishness or greed. Every time I want it, you fill my cup full, sometimes adding espresso giving me the burst that I need. You never hold back adding sweetness when desired; adding your own special something to keep me and my fire intensified. Just keep the caramel flowing and the coffee will soon follow, filling in all the voids and making solid my hard wood at times seems a bit hollow. All your ingredients so perfectly arranged, is it strange that I view you this way, a sweet cup of you to start my day. I end with you as well not wanting my cup to no time soon become empty. I savor every sip and compare you to none.

Dream Reality

Morning comes with the presence of you lying next to me, your smell, your aroma has filled the air, all I have dreamed about, talked about, even had visions about. Your presence making sure true, I gently kiss your forehead, my lips sink and expand from the resistance of the skull, yes it's real, yes it's you, all I have dreamed about, talked about, even had visions about. Rubbing your naked body as it lies still, admiring all the curves, lines, shapes, figures, your bodies like a maze I want to get lost and never be found. I want to explore every inch of you, gently kissing and caressing, letting no part of you go without attention, not to mention how you got me feeling right about now. Man this is some shit, but good shit, dam you hit my spot without even touching, oh wee, touching it. Is this the morning after or the night before I wake and you're no longer here, the difference I'm awake and it is oh so good to see you, you are all I have dreamed about, talked about, and even had visions about. It is you I have craved and longed for, the conversation intoxicating, stimulating parts of my body that normally have to be touched but your words run deep, touch ever so gently all the right spots, don't stop I like the sound of your voice, don't stop keep talking for the more you speak the weaker I get, my knees are trembling from verbal vibrations of your vocal chords. My head is spinning from world wind whispers of you saying relax it's me your dream come true, the one you have dreamed about, talked about, even had visions about.

Why can't you

Why can't you be like her, have her personality, her ways, and her thoughts? The way she would hold me closest to her heart being able to hear her heartbeat. That sweet sound calms my soul and gives me inner peace. Why can't you encourage me to climb mountains most would perceive to be impassible, but she makes those thoughts a reality but rarely do I get that from you. Why can't you be that silent pillar of strength there to guide when guidance is needed otherwise enjoy the ride regardless of the direction we are moving forward, as I look forward to that time when you will make a justifiable effort to be like her. I know you're not her and could never be her but you could be all the things that make me smile, have a voice that sends chills down my spine, have a way with words that send me into a state of meditation and the shine you give off from your presence radiates in ways only thought of in a three dimensional view point, the point I make to you is to just try to be like her. I need and want someone like my Mother.

Wild Thoughts...

So tempted you engaged in meaningful conversation to arouse a
sensation of a lustful imagination.
How can I entice you with deeds for words have no effect?
You react so effortlessly and gracefully turning down all
advances.
I'm romancing you, dancing with you, glancing into your eyes,
but it's all in my mind as I have created a vision of you, but
dreams do come true.
Maybe not without circumstance, a stance on all your convictions but
with little or no restrictions to me reaching out to you.
I'm allured by your mystery, your history has neither time nor space for
the present and future will engulf all.
Take this drink with me, sink with me into a place where we both
feel secure, no decoys needed for all signs have been heeded.
If only for one night, let me lure you, ensure you, secure you, adore
you, explore you, never ignore you, Damn you!

The Day!!!

Showing you how much I care, thanking you for the time we share.
Time so often cut short by a day not long enough to give back or take
away something I so eagerly want, but don't want the day to end as my
heart mends not from a broken heart but a worn out soul.
I give you mine as we build ours, take as you will my feelings not for
granted but be granted the opportunity to spend one more day, no
one more night, no fighting for another smile for it comes so
naturally as happiness shines through.
Your smile highlights my day, I know you have to leave but I want
you to stay, I say again you highlight my day.
Intimacy of our minds and our bodies will soon follow, being so
focused so not on me but you always on my mind.

Don't be alarmed

Don't be alarmed my love just reassured,
so much time has passed but love will endure.
Don't be alarmed if my voice has faded because through our voice a
bond was created.
Created not for the moment or just something to do, it's you I want,
it's you I pursue.
This is short and sweet and all so true, soon you'll see your passions
I'll subdue.

A Friend

A friend of mine is a friend forever.
If no spoken words we're still together.
Taking time to listen with an open ear, even when I'm sad you
still bring cheer.
In the midst of danger, you comfort me most, not saying a word
you neither brag not boast.
Your smile is like sunshine where there is never
light, your words like melodies all through the night.
Just be my friend, what's the meaning of friend?
Would I be describing you?
Is it your soft-spoken words or things you do?
A friend in pleasure, a friend in pain, a friend in darkness, a friend
to remain, remain close to me even though far apart, the feeling of
happiness is only the start.
The start of something beautiful, can you imagine that?
The times we sit, the times we walk, even short but sweet the time
may seem, the dream of true friendship could you imagine that?
2/13/97

Imagine ...

Imagine a situation although complicated but situated in a spot, is that your spot I touched as you clutched my hand so tight with all your might. Release, let go, I caress, no stress, all worries subdued as if queued, you were under the control of mine, my mind has wrapped around your body and soul, not to control but to release the beast as I feast on your innermost place, that taste, my face has become one, two, three dam release, you scream, I sigh as I look a sparkle in your eye, a glow on your face, your lips quiver ever so lightly, are you trying to say something, say something, it's only a dream.

Okay that's Alright!

Okay that's alright are words well spoken, a promise never made so none never broken.

My words bring about change if only for a little while.

Make me happy, make me smile.

Is it my charm or those soft-spoken words like a burst of silence soon to be heard?

My eyes wonder most when those words come out, make me jump around scream and shout.

Too many words spoken may soon get old; the charming words you use will sometimes touch my soul. They bring about action almost all the time, seeing a smile on your face makes my day shine.

Don't take these words just spoken and run away, hopefully my words will bring about action soon. What about today?

Through The Eyes of the Soul

Blackness So Beautiful

Nothing but blackness as I scan the crowd
Your Blackness so beautiful stands so proud
Flattering words nor dollars bills caught your eye nor turned your
wheels your face like a picture a thousand words spoken the frame
never tarnished, the glass never broken
I am the wind brushing against your outer most beauty I
am the air you breathe bringing life to your smile I am the
burst of energy you feel when in the mood I am the
tension reliever when passions are subdued
Let me render your blackness a charm
A precious jewel waiting to be revealed to the world whose eyes
have never seen the such.
Your Blackness so Beautiful
You can't feel it; you can't touch it a
feeling of being.

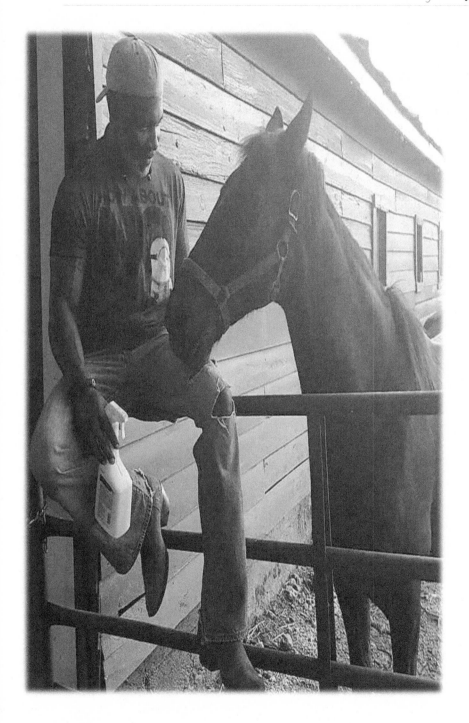

Through The Eyes of the Soul

Fire and Desire

My tongue so gently grazes your neck and nibbling on your ear not
knowing what to expect. My lips caress your body in spots only in a
dream, as I breathe down your spin, will you wiggle or will you scream.
Words become silence moans understood, the walls are not ladders
they'll do you little good. Feel the sensation of my hands cradling your
innermost beauty, I'm a man it's my duty.
My duty to protect and serve you until your heart and body can take no
more, like waters touching beaches and washing away the shore. A
sparkle of light (you) shines even in the midst of darkness, that gleam of
joy and passion a volcano waiting to erupt. The entrance of your passion
overflows with burning desire, a growing flame just goes higher and
higher. A flame so hot, water will freeze, winds will blow but without a
breeze. Mountains will crumble but still stand tall, valleys will deepen
and you still won't fall.

Fire and desire, actions not conversation,
the heat from your passion downright lust and infatuation.
12/21/97

I Miss You!

This sounds familiar you've heard it time after time, but if it wasn't so I wouldn't tell you I miss you. I miss you means I miss all of you, not just part, kind of like loving part of your soul and none of your heart. I miss the passionate kisses to get my motor going at the same time trying to stop my ManHOOD from showing. He stands at attention whenever you enter the room, when you're not around it seems like gloom and doom. I look high and oh so low to find someone like you to tell I miss, kiss, reminisce, thank God every day for the reason you exist. If you knew all you mean to me, would you shy away due to fright thinking he can't feel or miss me like this, no it's not right – it is, if you will just let it be, all I want is to be happy and free.

I miss YOU!

How Bout it!

How 'bout letting yourself be given and taken when release is release of mind and body. Grant you the choice to choose as you will my feel of you being felt by my hands alone but gone so far from your mind that I bring you back to that place which you so long, yearn and burn for. I feel your heart beat so close to mine that my mind may change upon request, you suggest I regress back to you for I fill you up with me, not half but all as we fall into a deep state of understanding, commanding our thoughts to become one but one has confusion with the illusion that things are not as they seem but they are what you think they are but we as one must conclude that we have pursued a course that once traveled will lead to a place of complete pleasure and satisfaction, your reaction gains traction as you hold on for the ride of a lifetime. How 'bout it ...

What If

What if I could tell you things and get your heart to
listen, wait a moment longer for your eyes to glisten.
Tell you I'm here when you are there, tell you I miss you and not
even care, not care about the words of the world and all they have
to say, care about the moment at hand and the rest of the day.
The night will soon come or do we continue our journey, the
journey of mystery and adventure just thinking about it makes me
horny.
I envision mountains high, valleys low, and flat plains out west; even
as the moon sets, it still has a glow. I envision your eyes plainly
focused on me and nothing else, me concentrating on you and
forgetting about self.
What if I gave you a key would you open up the door, or would
you kick it down without hesitation as our bodies connect and start
to explore?
Explore every inch, forget about the past and leave it where it lies
for it brings about pain and unwanted cries.
I want to release the pain and rain happiness on your
shoulders, lift the burden of life and carry it with honor.
I need you light as a feather as the wind so gently gets under your
wings and lifts you higher than you have ever been before, watch
you soar, watch you glide, watch you ride with a smile this thing
called life.

WE ARE!!!!

We are the ones that through basic conversation pick up on the needs, wants and desires and try to make those come to life.

We are the ones willing to put it all the line when consequences can end it all.

We are the ones wanting to see you at your best, even when others hope for failure. We are the ones that when we say we support you, even from afar, we are actually right next to you rooting you on as your biggest fan.

We are in no way a comparison or in competition with anyone else other than ourselves, as we are the Men wanting to please and that pleasure has brought us to this place of questioning our own actions but we will not change a thing and we will not reconfigure the respect as it relates to who we are.

We are the ones that used to take words thrown as weapons of destruction, now we view them as words of affirmation to be held accountable for actions shown.

We are the ones that put our flaws into context, showing that growth not excuses gives us the right to write another chapter.

We are the ones that recognize that mistakes can happen but choice was the ultimate decision maker not coincidence being used as selfish defense.

We are the ones that build lifelong bonds not fly by night connections that fizzle at first sign of confusion because the illusion was seen from every angle.

We are the ones that love deep, love strong, we are ones that our pain runs just as deep, just Respect US.
We are
Grown Ass Men.
T.D.

A Piece of Work ...

A Piece so transparent as what you see is what you get and words spoken are just as apparent, no filter needed as your smile provides creative flow of expressiveness for possessiveness is not a trait that has entered your blood stream. You are a conversation worth having with no topic being excluded. You are romance at a glance giving hope to the hopeless for love still exist and with a kiss it's made better and if distance separates us put it in a hand written letter and let me feel that endless glide of each stroke as your words resonate down to my core making me sore from all this twitching as if a current was flooding my most intimate body parts, I almost forgot you weren't present but your presence is felt. You are the interlude to a song never wrote, but has reached across the globe touching souls and reviving minds to be more than perceptions made. TBC ...
T.D.

Through The Eyes of the Soul

The Author

Though he'll forever be a Gulf Coast guy at heart, Timothy Duncan – author, poet, inspirational writer, and motivational speaker - now lives in Huntsville, Alabama. If he's not working on one of his latest mind provoking poems, you can find him either caring for and/or riding his horses, golfing, traveling and most importantly enjoying family and friends. He also enjoys watching movies and falling asleep before it gets to the good part only to wake up to say "what did I miss".

Tim is a true Renaissance Man. He has many interests and tries his best to be perfect with each one. His love of poetry and the many messages that he can conceive from one word or sentence, gives him even more drive to explore the minds of all he comes in contact with. He is able to express on paper the thoughts of many and can paint a picture that gives the reader the ability to see words in motion. Tim Duncan is excited with this project, his first venture into letting the world explore his thoughts or his perceptions of love,

"I write in my reality, my past, my future, and my truth. Maybe in your eyes it's all false but I write my desires, my wants, my needs, my expectations. I write what I see, what I want to see, what I've seen, what I've heard and with all that said, my poems will be what you make them – So how Deep are you willing to go"?

life and loss. He considers the release of *Through the Eyes of the Soul* to be one of his greatest accomplishments, besides getting a hole in one on the golf course.

Through the Eyes of the Soul is going to blow your mind with its sharp edges and a sensual heat, hot enough to melt steel. The poems are one man's raw interpretation of life - as its dealt, death, love, deceit, fantasy and fiction all packed in one small package talking to you *Through the Eyes of the Soul.*

Tim Duncan was raised in Daphne, a small rural town in south Alabama right across the bridge from Mobile (for those who know, will know). Growing up Tim along with his brothers were always active in sports and always staying busy and out of trouble for the most part. Tim learned early the value of hard work, earning spending money cutting grass with his grandfather. Tim, despite the loss of very significant people in his life, pressed forward leaving South Alabama to the most Northern part of the state - Huntsville Alabama - where he graduated from Alabama A&M University twice, first earning a Bachelor's degree in Marketing and later returning while working full-time to earn his M.B.A. Tim is a dedicated member of Omega Psi Phi Fraternity, Incorporated - Nu Epsilon Chapter. Ω

Made in the USA
Monee, IL
20 November 2021

82266879R00132